Jack **Gibson**
The Last Word

Jack **Gibson**
The Last Word

with Ian Heads

ABC
Books

The ABC 'Wave' device is a trademark of the Australian Broadcasting Corporation and is used under licence by HarperCollins*Publishers* Australia.

Dirst published in 2003
This paper edition published in 2008 by ABC Books
for the Australian Broadcasting Corporation.
Reprinted in 2010 by HarperCollins*Publishers* Australia Pty Limited
ABN 36 009 913 517
harpercollins.com.au

Copyright © Jack Gibson 2003

The right of Jack Gibson to be identified as the author of
this work has been asserted under the *Copyright Amendment
(Moral Rights) Act 2000*.

This work is copyright. Apart from any use as permitted under the
Copyright Act 1968, no part may be reproduced, copied, scanned,
stored in a retrieval system, recorded, or transmitted, in any form
or by any means, without the prior written permission of the publisher.

HarperCollins*Publishers*
25 Ryde Road, Pymble, Sydney, NSW 2073, Australia
31 View Road, Glenfield, Auckland 0627, New Zealand
A 53, Sector 57 Noida, UP, India
77–85 Fulham Palace Road, London W6 8JB, United Kingdom
2 Bloor Street East, 20th floor, Toronto, Ontario M4W 1A8, Canada
10 East 53rd Street, New York NY 10022, USA

ISBN 978 0 7333 2449 9

Produced by Geoff Armstrong
Set in 11/13 *Bembo* by Kirby Jones
Original cover design by Ninehundred VC, adapted by Kirby Jones
Cover image courtesy Newspix

CONTENTS

Author's Note ~ *vii*
Introduction ~ *ix*
Forewords ~ *xiii*

PART ONE
Jack Gibson ... In His Own Words

ONE When I Was Coach 3
TWO The Game 12
THREE Four Outstanding Teams 21
FOUR Talent is Secondary 25
FIVE Parents Have to Set the Example 31
SIX Motivation Comes From Within 35
SEVEN Coach Killers and Other Players 38
EIGHT A Team Sport 44
NINE The Front Office 47
TEN Fans 52
ELEVEN Facts of Life 55

TWELVE Nowhere to Hide   61

THIRTEEN Heroes   63

FOURTEEN One Game Closer to a Win   77

PART TWO
From the Jack Gibson Collection

ONE The Coach Says   83

TWO About the Coach   88

THREE Talking and Listening   92

FOUR Leadership   97

FIVE Building a Team   104

SIX Great Expectations   109

SEVEN The Best Advice   113

EIGHT Seats of Learning   116

NINE Facing Facts   124

TEN Persist!   130

ELEVEN Human Nature   139

TWELVE Forks in the Road   145

THIRTEEN Face the Music   152

FOURTEEN The Art of Coaching   158

FIFTEEN Proverbs   171

SIXTEEN Food for Thought   174

SEVENTEEN As Told by the Greats   189

Author's Note

Royalty proceeds from the sale of this book will go in equal shares to NISAD (Neuroscience Institute of Schizophrenia and Allied Disorders) and to the Mental Health Sports Association.

In the interest of translating some universal wisdom directly to the fields of sports coaching, leading and teaching, I have taken some licence in the pages that follow — and I trust those involved will forgive me for that.

The Last Word contains not only a collection of my own thoughts and beliefs and some of the things I've learnt in life, 16 seasons of first-grade rugby league coaching and two years with the New South Wales State of Origin team, but also the valued and valuable thoughts of hundreds of wise men and women, spanning many centuries. The second half of the book is the result of the continuation of a reading program that began for me when I first became a football coach, with Eastern Suburbs back in 1967. I realised fairly early that the 'wisdom of the ages' — whether from 3000 years ago or from yesterday — often was simply and perfectly adaptable to the context of the football arena, and immensely valuable. From my regular morning habit of reading, I would write down any wise, pragmatic and smart quotes and ideas that struck me, and that I felt could be of use in coaching.

In sharing in this book many hundreds of examples of the body of wisdom that I have gathered, I have, here and there, and for my own benefit, skewed the quote slightly by substituting the word 'coach' or 'coaching'. But I have always been careful to retain the exact meaning of what was originally intended. So it is that we have people all the way from Cato the Elder, through Napoleon Bonaparte to Albert Einstein and Thelonious Monk, joining many overseas gurus of sport and business in sharing their thoughts on sports coaching! My thanks go to all of them — those still here, those long departed, and also those whose words of wisdom, despite my best endeavours, appear in the book without attribution. I would suggest that we who choose to coach, to teach or who have pretensions of leadership in any field can learn from all of them. I know that I have.

The re-emergence of two audiotapes from 20 or more years ago, featuring interviews conducted when I was right in the thick of the cut and thrust of a career coaching first-grade football, provide an insight into my coaching philosophies and have provided some material for *The Last Word*. Thanks, belatedly, to two good media/league men — Frank Hyde and Richard Fisk — who interviewed me back then, and to Owen Denmeade, who thought enough of the interviews to file away the tapes all these years and then offered them for this book.

My special thanks also to the people who so generously contributed their thoughts in the forewords that lead us into the book. Together they make up one of the finest 'teams' of all my experience, and I am immensely appreciative of the kind words offered. My appreciation also goes to Ian Heads, who was writing league in the year that I began coaching and who worked with me, as he had on earlier books, on the putting together of *The Last Word*, and to Geoff Armstrong, whose enthusiasm for the project and diligence in shaping the book into what it became were invaluable.

Jack Gibson
June 2003

Introduction
By Ian Heads

Oracle, n. person or thing serving as infallible guide, test or indicator; authoritative, profoundly wise, mysterious adviser or advice, prophet.

— *The Concise Oxford Dictionary*

The phone at Jack Gibson's house, deep in the Sutherland Shire south of Sydney, still rings off the hook most days. The big man has been out of coaching for 15 years now, and 'officially' out of rugby league football altogether for almost a decade. But he is still 'The Oracle' — attracting an eclectic passing parade, seemingly non-stop, and which on a single day might range through highly paid, high-profile, first-grade coaches, to troubled footballers seeking guidance, on to newspapermen chasing an oblique quote to add depth and meaning to a story. Most come seeking a fragment of Gibson wisdom. Since Jack's legendary status was put firmly in place, especially through his towering achievements as coach of Eastern Suburbs (champions 1974, 1975) and Parramatta (1981, 1982, 1983), it has been ever thus.

The formula for *The Last Word* is as it was for Jack's previous books — the best-selling *Played strong, done fine* (1988), *Winning Starts on Monday* (1989) and *When all is said and done* (1994) — the sum of its pages providing an even wider view of the winning Gibson philosophy. One early morning in 2002, Jack rang me to say that he had gradually accumulated what he believed to be a body of worthwhile material ... and what did I reckon about having a look at it with the view to ... maybe ... a fourth book? I discovered that the material gathered by Jack in his 'bowerbird' morning mode was wise, quirky, funny and educational — collected doggedly from a huge variety of sources and meticulously penned in notebooks in Jack's looping hand.

'You never know where you're going to find wisdom and knowledge,' says Jack. 'There are no rules on that. Often in stuff far removed from football there is something relevant to coaching. When I find those things, I write them down.'

The Last Word grew from there. Its beginning lay in these hundreds of quotes and observations gathered since 1995. Via interviews with Jack and some enthusiastic digging in the archives, the development of the second 'leg' of the book — the adding of specific Jack Gibson content — then began. The ambition was that this material would personalise the current book and build on the philosophy laid down in his earlier works.

In long interviews conducted at his home, Jack ranged across football and footballers, coaches and cricket, winning and losing ... and life as he saw it. An old pal of Jack's from playing days long ago at Eastern Suburbs, Owen Denmeade, chipped in with forgotten interview tapes, recorded when Jack was at the height of his coaching powers. In one of them, legendary broadcaster Frank Hyde quizzes Gibson on the subject of winning and what it takes to succeed, before an audience of executives from the motor trade. A second interview, conducted 20 or so years ago by Richard Fisk (now Promotions & Media Manager for the Sydney Roosters), dug into various aspects of the Gibson philosophy. Columns written by Jack many years ago for the Sydney *Daily Mirror* and some quotes from *Rugby League Week* gave further valuable insights into the

Gibson Way, and added even more spice to the mix. A Mike Gibson interview for a video compiled by Graham 'Shadow' McNeice in the late 1980s was revisited, and some gems extracted.

The result is not a series of lengthy chapters in the 'traditional book' sense, but rather a collection of short, sharp 'jabs' of wisdom and football history, collected under a variety of themes, that together provide a revealing insight into Jack's highly successful — and unique — approach to coaching and life.

Hopefully this book will fill some more gaps in the long and continuing story of arguably the greatest football coach Australia has seen. A modest man, Jack said long ago he was not interested in writing a formal biography. But through his books, the beliefs and philosophies that have made him so successful, and changed very much for the better the lives of many footballers around him, are at least 'out there'. Often with Jack those beliefs are — in the one breath — a mix of the simple and the profound and very often they are messages that are about a lot more than just football. They are about such things as people making the most of themselves, of the wisdom of treating fellow human beings with respect, of playing fairly and winning graciously … and of losing the same way.

The Last Word, like Jack's previous books, has been created for the good of other people — with earnings from sales going in full to support beloved causes into which Jack and Judy Gibson have put so much energy, such as research into the causes and treatment of schizophrenia. With Jack 74 now and his health edging just a little below where he would like it to be, there is a temptation to suggest that this book represents the completion of a 'Gibson Quartet'. But don't put up the correct weight flag on that just yet — even if he's half a yard slower than he once was, Jack remains a searcher for wisdom. There is no reason to doubt that his hunt will continue, and that maybe sometime down the track there'll be another phone conversation which begins with the words: 'I don't know if you're interested … but I've got a few things here that might make a book.'

The so-called Great Coaches have been among the most unusual and most outstanding products of Australian sport over the years. They are not always the 'easiest' of people, but there is no doubt that the likes of Ric Charlesworth (hockey), Don Talbot (swimming) and Wayne Bennett (rugby league) have been, and are, great *teachers*, too; able to lift and inspire the athletes around them, to provide their people with the ground rules for success, and thus to steer them towards successful lives after sport.

So it is with Jack Gibson. The diverse opinions offered in the forewords penned for this book add up to a clear and valuable picture of his uniqueness in sport's wide world. And via the varied and often witty utterances of 'Coach Jack', and then from the people he reads and admires, I hope readers can take from the pages that follow some wisdom and inspiration for their own lives.

Ian Heads
May 2003

Postscript

Jack Gibson died at 6.32pm on Friday, May 9, 2008, 90 minutes before the Centenary Test match between Australia and New Zealand kicked off at the Sydney Cricket Ground. He was 79 and had been in fading health in the last years of his life. Jack was by then officially rugby league's 'Coach of the Century', elevated to that honour at a gala dinner the previous month. His death prompted a flood of stories, tributes and memories. In a farewell penned for *The Sunday Telegraph*, May 11, I wrote the following words, trying to capture the essence of this man of many parts: 'Jack Gibson, Kiama-born on February 27, 1929, schooled in the University of Life, was a giant – the great coach and teacher of the game of rugby league and, more than that, one of the outstanding and most influential figures of all Australian sport.'

He was all of those things, and much more, and the tributes flowed for days as people remembered 'Big Jack'.

Forewords

By Wayne Bennett

Jack Gibson was my role model in coaching. As a young coach in Brisbane in the late 1970s, I admired him from afar, admired everything he stood for. And what he stood for was the players, and for the game. Of all the coaches over the years, he was the great innovator. He studied the American game because they were way ahead of us at that time — and identified methods and ideas that he knew would work in rugby league. So many things that we coaches now take for granted were Jack Gibson innovations. As far as I am concerned he gave football coaching credibility, and took coaching to a new level. And what he did he did in an unassuming way. He never gave himself a pat on the back for it. It was because of Jack that people started to realise that coaches *do* make a difference.

I first met Jack in 1979. I was coaching Southern Suburbs in Brisbane, and had been there since '77. That year (1979), we had come from last the year before to win a place in the preliminary final. Souths had not been in a grand final since 1953, and we had to beat Des Morris' Eastern Suburbs to get there.

Jack Astill, chairman of Souths Juniors, said to me one day: 'Wayne, what can I do for this team? How can I help you?' I told him I would love to get Jack Gibson up to Brisbane for the night, just to talk to the guys. So a few phone calls were made and, unbelievably, Jack came. I probably do a fair bit of that myself these days — you know, just turn up at a place where people don't really expect me to be. On the night before the final in '79, Jack spoke to the team and he was great. He showed a video called *The Value of Preparation* and stayed on and had dinner with us. And I remember him saying, in his offbeat way, certainly not big-noting: 'You'll win tomorrow, but I can't get back next week to help you ... so you'll be in a bit of trouble.' He was right. We won the final, against all the odds, but got beaten in the grand final.

That meeting with Jack was the beginning of a link which has grown into a very strong friendship. When I went to the Canberra Raiders as a young coach in 1987, he was the first to welcome me — via a phone call wishing me all the best in the Sydney comp. I remember him speaking at a dinner before a Canberra game one day and someone asked him about selectors. In that dry way of his he answered, 'Selectors? In America, when they talk about selectors, they're talking about what you have in the gearbox of your car.' He changed all that for coaches. With Jack, if he was going to coach the side, he was going to carry the responsibility. He was going to live and die by what *he* did, and not kowtow to three or four selectors picked by a committee. As Ron Barassi said to me one day, Jack was the first coach to declare what he wanted.

He was the master motivator, although he probably doesn't see himself in that role. He doesn't go on with a lot of stuff, but what he says is often profound and has the effect of making you think a little about yourself. There are some who believe that to motivate people you have to make a half-hour speech. But you don't, and Jack always understood that. He didn't make great speeches, but what he said, he meant, and it cut right to the bone. I love the story of his speech when Parramatta won their first premiership, in 1981 after 34 years in the competition. He got up on stage and said, 'Ding dong, the witch is dead.' That was all. If he had talked for an hour everyone there that night would have long forgotten his words by now. But everyone remembers 'Ding dong, the witch is dead'. The monkey was off Parramatta's back; it could not possibly have been put any better.

The other side of Jack Gibson is that he's such a generous man. What he has done for charity is huge. He cares about people, and he's always doing something for someone. More than once he has offered me some time on his farm. 'You look tired, coach,' he'll say. 'Do you want to have a break? Go down to the farm for a few days?'

Maybe there are people who don't know it, because it's a fair while ago now, but Jack got me the coaching job at the Brisbane Broncos in 1988. All the directors of the new club made the trek down to Sydney to see him, and Jack just looked them in the eye and said: 'If you want your club to head in the direction that you hope it can there is only one guy for the job.'

I'm told they all looked at each other and asked, 'Who's that?'

And Jack said, 'Wayne Bennett.'

When someone mentioned that I was tied up at Canberra, Jack brushed it aside. 'You can fix that,' he said.

Fifteen years later I'm still at the Broncos and I hope I haven't disappointed him. He's a man I would never want to let down.

A big man, Jack made an impact on coaching and rugby league that was nothing short of huge. The rest of us have just followed and, I hope, made him proud of us as coaches, making our own way along the trail he blazed. He didn't go down the beaten track, he cut his own path. Those of us who have followed have maybe made a bit of difference in our own ways, but it was Jack who gave us the credibility and gave us the strength to be different. He was the pioneer and through the progress made in the years since I know that today's coaches in rugby league are the equivalent of any coaches in any sport in the country.

Jack has never changed. He remains a modest and humorous and decent man, and I am delighted that the words that underpin his philosophy have been gathered in this book. There is a small story that to me says so much about him. When I launched my own book last year, we invited Jack and he came along. I felt very humbled. And at the end he came and stood in a longish queue and asked me to sign a book for him. The truth was that I would have walked 100 miles to sign a book for Jack! But there he was in the line, not looking for any favours and not wanting to put himself in front of anybody else. I remember putting my arm around him later and saying, 'Jack, you didn't have to get in line.'

And he just looked at me and said, 'It's okay, Wayne.'

By Michael Cronin

On Grand Final day 1980, I ran into Jack at the SCG and he asked me a simple question: 'What do you want out of football?' I told him that I wanted to win a premiership. On the same day two years later, after Parramatta had made it back-to-back grand final wins under Jack's coaching, he came up to me in the dressing room. 'Got greedy, eh?' he said.

These three words summed up at least two of Jack's special qualities: his humour, which was (and is) never far from the surface and which made it a true enjoyment to play under him, and also the steel-trap Gibson mind. Until that day in September '82 we had never discussed what I had told him back in 1980. But he hadn't forgotten.

I first met Jack in 1974, on a golf course. I was in the Australian side, and a few of us — Arthur Beetson, Bob Fulton and Ron Coote from memory — had a round of golf one day. Jack, whose reputation as an outstanding coach was already well established, was there too, having arrived in his big American car. Back then, I was a young footballer from the 'bush' and still pretty overawed by most things, and after we'd been out on the course for a good while he said to me: 'You don't say much, do you?' I was thinking, 'Well, we've been out here for a couple of hours and I haven't heard *you* say too much either.'

Jack was having trouble with his putting that day. I recall he was using a two iron on the greens, and I was kicking the thought around that here was a bloke having trouble coaching himself. Back then I only *thought* such things; today, knowing him as I have come to, I would say them!

It was an experience to play under Jack's coaching for three years at Parramatta (1981 to 1983), something I value greatly. We had great success and plenty of fun, too. As coach, Jack tended to keep us guessing a bit, and now and then he'd come up with moves that were completely different. One of them was the 'Wall' — where a number if players lined up, with their backs to the opposition, to disguise our attacking play that was unfolding. It received a lot of publicity. For a time there was this additional thing with it, whereby we players all had to look up into the sky when the Wall was set — in line with the premise that when someone stops and looks up into the air ... everyone stops and looks up.

Before a semi-final in one of the premiership years, Jack came up with a planned move in which Peter Sterling would kick the ball 20 metres across the field to me, standing flat-footed in the centres. I was thinking: can anything good possibly come out of this? We practised it and practised it and then, in the last training session before the semi, Jack canned it. With experiences like that, I was never quite sure whether his real motivation was simply to keep us thinking.

For a while in his first year at Parramatta we adopted an American idea where the first bloke onto the field would clap the next in line out, then the first two would clap the third, and so on. Before long, Jack got the drift that we players weren't too happy with this, so again he canned it. That was the way he operated. He'd try something out, but if it didn't work he'd drop it.

Jack's mixture of humour, vagueness and astuteness kept life interesting at all times. His is an interesting mind. A lot of the time with Jack you get the impression he's thinking about something else. And often he is ... and he isn't. At the first Parramatta training session in 1981, he started working us on a move, then wandered off somewhere. Eventually he came back. 'Now, where was I up to?' he asked in his vague way. At training, he'd say things like: 'The boy Ella ... where is he?' Steve Ella would be standing straight in front of him.

But Jack was also a great provider of opportunity for players. As with tactics he tried in football matches, he'd give people chances but he wouldn't carry them if it wasn't working out. His theory was that if you were calling out one bloke's name too often, spending too much time on an individual, then everyone else would be suffering. He looked for people who wanted to play. I remember him saying to reserve-grade coach John Monie one day, when Monie was based on the Central Coast: 'Have you got any blokes up there who can play? I don't care if they're young or old or big or small, as long as they can play.'

Jack always coached to his side's strengths. And he kept it simple. He never asked a player to do something he thought he couldn't do. He'd give him basic instructions and then let the good players take over. If he had sides that could attack, then he let them attack, but if he had sides that weren't so flash, then he'd work on their defence, because he knew that that part of their game had to be good. Jack realised long ago that rugby league was a simple game, so he coached that way. Meanwhile, others tried to complicate it ...

As I found out on the golf course that first day I met him, Jack doesn't waste words. It was that way on match day. During a game at Belmore Sports Ground, when we were going extra well, he came into the dressing room at halftime, looked us over, and said: 'You blokes probably know more about this game than I do. Just keep doing what you're doing.' That was it.

Only once did I see him blow up on the whole team. That was at halftime in a night game against Penrith. We had been nothing short of disgraceful in the first 40 minutes and deserved what he delivered to us. At other times, though, he did blow up individuals, but even these instances were rare. In one of prop Geoff Bugden's first games for Parramatta, Jack decided to replace him. Geoff obviously wasn't impressed and as he left the field he grabbed the walkie-talkie that linked Jack in the coach's box to his staff on the sideline. 'Why am I being taken off?' Geoff demanded. I was nearby and immediately thought, 'Hmm ... bad move that.'

Jack's answer was brief: 'I'll talk to you on Tuesday.' He did.

Jack was very seldom wrong. And even if you happened to think he was, the inclination — once you got to know him — was to accept his advice. Players came to accept his decisions in the certain knowledge that he wasn't there to make a mug of them. As coach, he was fair-minded at all times. If you were No. 55 at the club or No. 1, you were treated the same. At club meetings, he'd always single out a few of the senior blokes, just so the other players would feel that everyone was getting the same treatment. I have always understood since those Parramatta days that any young person in sport who happens to find a coach like Jack is extremely fortunate.

Of course, the thing with Jack was that it was never just about football; it was always about a whole lot more than that. He had certain standards he believed in and upheld, and certain beliefs about life, about the way things worked, and about the way people should conduct themselves. His influence and work have gone a long way beyond football. I don't think anyone could begin to guess how much effort, time and financial support he has given to various charities over the years.

And, with Jack, it's the small things that are just as special as the big achievements. So many times, he's turned up at functions when no one expected him to arrive, helping out more people than any of us know or could imagine. Not long back, a bloke from down my way on the NSW South Coast, who coached a junior side that had been really struggling despite all the effort being put in, asked Jack if he could perhaps do some little thing for the kids in the team. Jack requested the names of all the players, found out a little bit about each one, and then presented each of them with a book in which he had written a quote that he believed was applicable to the young recipient.

I am fortunate that my career as a player coincided with Jack's as a coach. I have no doubt that that chance event helped me as a footballer, and helped me outside football as well. He has not only been a positive presence in my life, he's been a true friend.

By Judy Gibson

Jack and I have been together 48 years now. It's been a sporting life, and I reckon I've been a good sport! We met through football, at a cabaret at the NSW Leagues Club in Phillip Street, and we got married when I was 21, so I've been married to him for more than two-thirds of my life. When you look at it that way ... my God!

I think one of the secrets of our long life together lies in the different roles we took, and sometimes in the different directions our interests took us. As a coach, Jack was probably fortunate that he could focus fully on his football. He didn't have a formal timetable to live to, or a business to run, and the way it worked out, I took over the family role and allowed him whatever time he needed to do his job. I knew it was important for him to do that, to follow his dream. And for me to have him as a happy person, doing what he wanted to do and succeeding at it, that was better for me and the family in the long run. I never begrudged him going out to training, or doing what he did. Being married to someone like Jack, you can't sit at home and wish you were there. You have to get out and find interests for yourself, and I have done a lot of things through my life. I believe the sort of independence we've had is healthy, as long as you end up in the same place.

At Royal Easter Show time in the early years, I'd stay home with the baby (and we always seemed to have one of those) and he'd take our elder kids out to the Show. They'd start with the animals and then go to everything else, including Jimmy Sharman's boxing tent, all the rides, all the sideshows. And he'd take the kids camping, down to Garie Beach, in the Royal National Park, south of Sydney. That's another of the secrets of our life together — I didn't have to go to the Show and I didn't have to go camping! I'd just happily wave them goodbye.

During Jack's time in football, as a player and then a coach, football was our social life, too. We met some terrific people and made some wonderful friends.

In his years as a coach, Jack was always searching for that edge. He was aware that success is transient, that it is difficult to stay a winner. He knew the essence of how to get there, but he knew too that to stay there took something extra. And when he moved on he never wanted to leave a club in worse shape than he found it. That was a very basic thing in him when it came to coaching; if he could come away from a club thinking he had done them no harm, even if they hadn't won anything, he was happy enough with that. As a coach, he was always keen for his players to have a job, to be occupied in their lives. I think he always understood that in life you've got to have a pattern, and some strong discipline, and that belief was a foundation of what he did as a coach.

The reading he has done, and all the collected material that has become this book and the ones before, were (and are) part of his search for the 'edge'. A lot of the material he accumulated in the early years was in a football vein, ideas that he could use in his own coaching. He read a lot of stuff, seeking things that he felt would sharpen him. He was never the sort of man to sit down and read a book for three or four hours. But he's a *consistent* reader, and he's read as much or more than most people in his different way, in sifting through books and newspapers and magazines. He has gathered philosophies that are worthwhile, ideas he knew would be of some worth in his field of football coaching. I knew it was happening, yet I didn't really know. He'd just be writing all these things down, and the only hint I would get might be an occasional: 'Jude, listen to this!'

After football, this collecting passion widened. Jack had more time on his hands and I found myself having to work my way around the collectable items that would arrive at home after auctions. He became something of a bowerbird, all of it centred around the charities that he, and I, supported. That started as long as 30 years ago, when Jack bought a house in Cronulla to be used as a 'halfway house' by the drug rehabilitation group, WHOS (We Help Ourselves). All these years later, WHOS is still going, although based much closer to the city these days.

Jack has an eye for interesting things. He's been a lover of good paintings from a long while ago, and even opened up a little gallery with his brother-in-law at one stage. But it was after football that the collecting really started, in the same way that he collected quotes in his reading. At different times, we've had just about everything you could ever think of in the house: antique golf clubs, old guns, typewriters, boxing memorabilia, cash registers, gramophones, cameras. He even bought me a chastity belt from the 19th century, complete with key. I don't think he meant me to wear it.

It seemed that the things that interested Jack interested others too. It would be impossible to estimate just how much money has been raised for charities via Jack's passion for collecting unusual things over the years.

People have said to me that they believed Jack was more than a football coach, that he was a teacher too. I think that's true — a good coach *is* a good teacher in the wider sense. But I don't think Jack would ever have possessed the tolerance for formal teaching. However, if you define a teacher as someone who is able to pass on information that is of value, then I'm sure he has been that.

By Alan Jones

Well, the biographies of Jack Gibson will tell us that he played prop for Eastern Suburbs, which he did from season 1953 to 1961. His playing career over, he was there, looking on, when his old club failed to win a game in 1966. But as Easts new coach in 1967, he took them to the semis.

The biographies will say that he then coached St George in the 1971 Grand Final, only to be beaten by Souths. It will continue to record that in 1973 he coached Newtown to their first and only club championship and to the semi-finals of the competition, at a time when the tribal nature of Sydney rugby league was at its zenith. But Newtown, too, were beaten.

So it was back to Easts … and those elusive premierships arrived in 1974 and 1975, the latter producing the biggest belting in Grand Final history: 38–0 over St. George. Then a brief sabbatical and on to Parramatta in 1981. Jack's three years there brought three premierships, the longest premiership winning streak since the great St. George era.

So much for biography …

'Biography' is, in relation to Jack Gibson, an imperfect statement of the nature and worth of the man. As a rugby league coach, he revolutionised the game. He brought innovation in training techniques, in selection and in playmaking, which became the benchmark for coaches and players down through the years.

A laconic exterior masked a tough and steely resolve within. He wasn't frightened by challenge; nor was he overcome by circumstance; nor was he intimidated by convention. Some of his team and positional selections are legendary, and the successes as a result of them, equally so.

But in many ways it was off the football field, as much as on it, that Jack will be remembered. There are any number of young men, not so young today, who will say that they owe their success in life to the example and instruction provided by Jack Gibson. He was the sort of bloke who I envisaged saying metaphorically to some young charge, 'Always put something in the collection plate.'

Jack was a firm believer that if you did something good, there would be a far greater return. But only after effort and application.

'Gibbo' made a reputation for talking slowly, but will always be remembered by those who know him for thinking quickly. What often appeared to be a genial and gentle observation about life invariably contained truisms that will stay with the listener all his life. We remember his famous instruction to the great Peter Sterling. 'Kick to the seagulls,' Jack told him at the Sydney Cricket Ground, 'because where the seagulls are, the players ain't.'

Now everybody kicks to the seagulls. 'Kick to land, not hand,' some now say, or, 'Play into space.' These are variations on the Gibson rule.

But Gibbo was never bound by rules. He was the bloke who always gave the impression that he believed you should learn the rules, but if you were to win, you might have to break some. And he did — in training, in selection, in defining what represented a team.

A team to him was more than the players. A team was the player and his father, his family, his education and his personal health. Without these, raw ability was never going to get anyone far at all.

Gibbo was demanding. He didn't settle for compromise. There is an awful word used about sport today called 'focus'. You hear about players being 'focused' without too many people knowing what it means. I think Jack would be saying to his players, instead of, 'Stay focused', something like, 'Don't let weeds grow around your dreams.'

He wanted young people to dream. And he offered himself as the agent for the realisation of those dreams.

He never allowed anyone to enter the comfort zone. It was exciting to the world outside, but demanding for those within. Jack Gibson taught young people that great achievements involve great risk. That's why his teams were regarded as among the best attacking sides in history. Not for him the boring conservatism of much of the modern game.

And another thing ...

Gibbo gave the impression that neither he, nor those in his charge, ever took anything for granted. Just as in life, you must never take good friends, good health or good circumstances for granted in training and in playing. Gibbo believed that you had to work at it, work at it and work at it over and over again, lest you make untidy assumptions about what you are capable of doing.

Now, of course, all we can do is look back. And when we do we see an inspirational person, a successful human being and a loyal and worthy friend.

It's the nature of coaches to talk a lot, to sermonise. I think Jack Gibson is one of the old brigade who believed that a good example was the best sermon. In all that he did and with all those he supervised, Jack was that good example.

By Ron Massey

I am honoured and proud to have been a friend of Jack Gibson for almost 50 years. Throughout that time, Jack has been a fine family man, a great worker for charities and has given support to his many friends.

Jack was a fine sportsman. He represented NSW at rugby league, played first-grade cricket for Waverley and played golf off a handicap of two.

More than 30 years ago, when Jack told me he was going to have a shot at rugby league coaching, I started laughing and told him he was kidding. How wrong I was. He went on to become the greatest league coach of all time. I was fortunate to be what others kindly called his 'right-hand man'. The coaches of today owe so much to his drive and determination and pioneering ways — his laying down of a path that provided those who came later with every opportunity to be successful.

The opposition to coaches having the power to be in charge of their own destiny was extremely strong until Jack changed it all. Before Jack, a coach joining a club inherited a panel of selectors and assistant coaches hired by the committee of the club. The credentials of some of them to hold those important positions may have been that they had sold more tickets than anyone else in the weekly chook raffle, or they happened to be related to another member of the committee. Sadly, it was often not for their knowledge of football. Jack, through the perseverance that he is noted for, changed all this, resulting in coaches having the power to choose their own staff and giving them for the first time the right to be the masters of their fate.

In 1975, when he was coach of Easts, Jack introduced what I believe to be the best tool a coach has: the video. In those days, videos were in black and white and came with so much snow on the screen that it was difficult at times to distinguish between Arthur Beetson and Bunny Reilly. How much better it is these days, with push-button control, sharp colour images, stop frame, zoom and all the other extras.

Jack was the first coach to introduce defensive tackling drills at training, and the use of tackle counts in a match. In 1977, he was appointed coach of the Queensland Country team and at the first training session at Lang Park introduced his players to big tyre tubes, to be used for tackling practice. Sitting in the grandstand as a spectator at training that day was the famous Queensland coach (and former champion player), Duncan Thompson. Afterwards, he sent one of his groundstaff over to ask if I could spare him a couple of minutes. I happily obliged, being only too pleased to meet such a legend of our game. Duncan wanted to say to me how exciting it was for him to see, for the first time, tackling drills used at training. How different it is at football training sessions now!

Much has been written and spoken about Jack's ability as a coach and as a motivator of sportspeople and others. It is a fact that virtually every footballer Jack coached became a better player. And I am just as certain that every player he came into contact with became a better person too, after experiencing his advice and direction.

Indeed, in my view, Australia has become a better place for the role he has played over the years, under a title he does not like but which sums him up: Jack Gibson, super coach … and super person.

By John Singleton

Australian sport is made up of two groups of people. Those who are friends of Jack Gibson and those who wish they were.

In his career as a player, coach, observer of men — both their strengths and weaknesses — Jack has made an art form of editing 1000-word essays into three-word quips. Like most men of great talent, Jack dismisses his own gifts and treasures the lesser talents of others.

So, while most of us are reading the business and sports pages of newspapers, Jack is reading books. And for the 30 odd — really odd — years I have known him, Jack has fastidiously kept the best observations and quotes of others in scrapbooks. Each written in his own perfect copperplate handwriting, just so he wouldn't forget.

This book is therefore not only a collection of the wisdom of Jack, continuing and enlarging upon what we have shared in his other books, it is also a book of collected wisdom from others that Jack has used to learn from.

Me, I prefer the way Jack puts things to Aristotle or Churchill (Winston, not Clive). But if it is good enough for our greatest coach to draw inspiration from, then it will do me.

Like Jack's other books, I see *The Last Word's* greatest value in life lessons. Not just sport lessons.

Jack has often told me that he could always learn something from everyone. No exceptions, 'even the drunk in the corner'. Which is probably why Jack gets me to write forewords to his books. So for those of you who ever wondered where Jack got all that rare, condensed wisdom and insight from, read this book.

Who said this? 'If you're gonna steal, steal the best.'

I don't know, but I bet Jack does.

PART ONE

JACK GIBSON
In His Own Words

'Ideally, a player should play for himself. Aim to achieve something for himself. The fact is that you can't contribute to a team unless you satisfy yourself …'

JACK GIBSON, 2003

ONE

When I Was Coach

'It's not where you are today that counts.
It's where you are headed ...'

I remember a couple of hurdles I had to face when I was a player. One particular game, I had a problem and the coach tried to make it disappear for me by saying it didn't exist. But it *did* exist in my mind, so I thought, 'Well, I must be weak.' The coach's response took my confidence. He didn't understand enough about the job he'd given me. He couldn't coach; I couldn't play.

• • •

When I was coach, I had to have plenty of authority. It wasn't that I was automatically going to use it, but I had to have it. The players had to know that I had it — that if I wanted to cut them or fine them or drop them I could — but I also needed people around me who could have their say. It was my team, but I needed the contributions of the other coaches at the club, my closest advisors, the statistician. There were always things that I'd miss: often, after a game, I'd think that a player hadn't had a great game, but when I looked at the stats I'd discover that he hadn't been penalised, hadn't committed any personal fouls, hadn't lost the ball, no bad passes, come up with a big tackle count. My opinion had to change.

> **'I'm still learning. I'll be confronted with circumstances this year that will be new to me.'**
>
> Jack after being appointed Cronulla coach, 1985. The Sharks were the sixth club he had coached (after Easts, St George, Newtown, Souths and Parramatta) since he began with Roosters in 1967.

I never coached Australia, and never regretted that fact. Whenever I could have coached Australia, I always had another job, and I never had the talent — and it is a talent — to be involved in two teams at the one time. And that's not me being a loyalist to my club; I just couldn't have handled it.

I would have liked to have that skill to split my time and thinking between two roles. But if I was with an Australian team I'd have been thinking about my club team and if I'd been with my club, I'd have been thinking about the Australian job. I couldn't adapt, some people can. There's nothing wrong with two jobs, far from it, but one job is enough for me. Because I always found that that one team is never off your mind.

The coach has to abandon everything else during the season; he's just got to work out a way not to get beat and he's doing that 24 hours a day. He's got to work out which pieces of advice he's going to listen to — which advice is good, what should be ignored. What's going to happen on Sunday is continually on the mind.

•••

When the player gets beat, he sweats the defeat out. He comes off, physically busted and mentally shot after an 80-minute football game, but if he thinks he's played to his talent then he can accept the defeat.

Meanwhile, the coach has got to do it cold turkey. He can't shower down because he hasn't played. He's got to overcome that sinking feeling before he can look at the video and make some sensible decisions about what he's going to do next week and come up with another strategy for not getting beat.

●●●

The coach's main job is not to win football games. That's on the list. The coach's main job is to keep quality in the joint, peace in the place, to keep opportunity in the place, and to be well managed. Probably also very high on the list is the coach's obligation to the game.

●●●

The most important lesson for a coach to learn is that you must have the authority to work to your potential. It's no good having the responsibility without the authority. Without authority, you will never know if you have the talent to coach. You have to have the authority to make decisions without a committee meeting.

In the US, a coach lives and dies on his team's performances. And I mean 'dies'. And so he should. He makes the decisions, he chooses the side for each game. To some degree, that was how I originally fell out with Easts in the late '60s … and how I fell out with some other clubs, too. They weren't prepared, weren't professional enough, to realise — as I did — that a coach must have complete control of a side.

For me, it got to the stage where I knew I could never work at a club where a bunch of selectors sat down to pick the teams on a Tuesday night.

●●●

The player has to be aware that you're prepared to give him the opportunity to succeed. If he's aware of that, he works. In reverse, I have to be aware he's doing the same for me — giving me the opportunity to succeed in the job that I do. We don't even have to like each other.

●●●

Coaches have to be a special breed of people.

How could it be that the job you fight to get and maintain can be so crooked on you? Personally, I liked the job as a coach. Why didn't the job like me?

The day of the game has no relaxed enjoyment whatsoever for the coach. For me, it was the most unhealthy day of the week. I didn't eat. I did drink black coffee, smoked too much (I don't smoke any more) and after the game I had my dessert, which consisted of a few beers.

If I happened to win, I'd smile occasionally, remembering the positive image the coach is supposed to possess.

If I lost, all that goes out the window.

●●●

There is one commodity a coach needs — time.

●●●

One of the hardest parts of a coach's job is watching the video replay of the game on Monday morning, knowing nothing will change. You still get beat ...

●●●

Video film of a football game has many and varied uses. For the coach it is the No. 1 aid.

Many times after a game I thought certain players had provided sub-standard performances. But after watching video that opinion was proved wrong. The opposite happened, too.

The quality of a player's contribution to team performance is easily assessed using video. The video never showed me any lies or distorted the facts. It showed me where the referee had made mistakes, sometimes in our favour and sometimes to our disadvantage.

The video doesn't talk back, it doesn't argue, it has no opinion. It records the facts as it sees them. It's up to the viewer to observe.

The video has only limited use for the person with limited opinion.

The innocent haven't much to fear from recorded evidence.

●●●

What you have to do is rely on your commonsense. The coach with the most commonsense prevails. He has to rely on that.

●●●

I'm sure a coach can overcoach a side. There's a lot of ways to make mistakes. My main thing as a coach was to make sure I didn't do the players any harm. A coach is there to give players opportunity. The real accolade for a coach is to get someone to a standard that they hadn't reached before.

●●●

You can't cover every point so don't try.

●●●

For a coach to raise his voice to his players is to admit he's lost it. It's a sign of panic — and that's contagious. A coach has to explain to his players that they can accomplish something, that it's going to get tough out there and that they're going to get frightened, but that they've got to react positively to all that. A coach must have confidence. I never had a team that walked out onto the field that I didn't think would win the football game. Sometimes, though, I did have to have a 'rethink' later.

●●●

They say that coaches coach what they couldn't do.

●●●

If you've got the balance between the physical and mental sides of football right then the team's going to benefit. It's one of the keys. You've heard of coaches after matches saying how things 'didn't feel right' in the dressing room before the game. Yeah, I've felt that. And that vibe always surrounds the coach. In such instances, the coach should get out of the room.

In 1985, Gibson agreed to coach Cronulla, and the great Steve Rogers, who had played the previous two seasons at St George, agreed to rejoin the club. At one of their first meetings as player and coach, Rogers (who had played centre, five-eighth and lock with the Dragons) asked Gibson what position he might be playing with the Sharks. To which Gibson replied ...

'I'll scratch where it itches.'

If you can keep it simple under pressure there's a good chance you're going to get the job done.

• • •

A coach has got to give his players the opportunity. I couldn't motivate anybody, but I could say: 'If you do this, these are your rewards, this is what will happen to you. If you don't, these are the negative things that can happen to you.' After that, I left it to the individual. From there, he had to do it himself. The coach can't do it for him, he can only advise — coaching is teaching the plus things and the minus things.

• • •

When I was a coach, I was concerned about my image, same as anybody else. But more important for me was that I had to do things my way, the way I saw as right.

I had to make a decision about what things I had to do, evaluate right from wrong, and do it the way it had to be done. My job was to do the best that I was capable of and work hard, harder than the other coaches. My players expected that of me. I had to keep on going.

• • •

Just because something works for somebody else doesn't necessarily mean it's going to work for you, but if I saw something working really well in another sport and I was keen about it, then I thought, 'It'll work for me.' But you make a lot of decisions throughout a season and you make plenty of mistakes. You only hope that you're pretty quick on recognising the things that don't work for you.

I'm always trying to investigate other areas and other sports, finding out what might work in rugby league. I think I've had times when things have gone for me and there have been other times when things I've tried haven't worked. It's a plus and minus thing; you play it as you see it.

• • •

I think my greatest failure as a coach was that at times I compromised with players. Maybe I shouldn't have.

A coach is in a position where he has to make decisions, to put people in and leave people out. Any decision I made, I always had to ask myself: 'What does it mean to the player that I put in?' When I compromised, I usually did it to avoid the big ruckus that would come from the player on the negative side of a decision. I was wary of losing him for future days. But that's all part of the scene.

If I had to cut a player, I needed to be, had to be, direct with him ... I'm not using you this week, but if you're smart enough you'll get your position back. They might not accept it straightaway, but the smart ones, when they go home and think about, then they will. One thing I stood by always: if ever I dropped a bloke who had a history of being a pretty good player, I made sure that I didn't put a mug in his place. I had to put a tough individual in his place. I owed that dropped player that.

• • •

From time to time, I'd go with a player who was unknown outside the club, but that was never a gamble so long as their record showed that what they'd done in their training was a positive, that their attitude through the season had been positive, that their clubmates liked them, that they were contributing, coachable. All these things were evaluated before we used them. If we had a player who was going good — irrespective of his age, weight or size — we liked to try to keep his momentum going. Such players told us by their attitude that they were ready, and once they were ready we wanted to use them. And as I've said before, if they're getting better we don't know how good they're going to get.

'Never be last out of a pub.'

— One of the 'simple rules' Jack insisted on when he was coach.

From time to time I'm asked who is the best coach in the game today. I answer this way: 'Well, you see, I don't have any experience under their coaching.' But I think the calibre of coaching in the game today is tremendous, has been for 20 years.

• • •

Rugby league coaches today have more individual responsibility than any other 10 people put together, because they're dealing with people — players, fans, media and administrators and all the conflicting personalities — all the time. The NRL must cooperate with them in all decision-making that has anything to do with the game at all. Back in my day, coaches' opinions weren't considered. They did stage a couple of get-togethers involving referees and coaches, but that was just an exercise in PR — I can't recall many of the coaches' suggestions ever being adopted. The authorities should listen to the coaches and get their ideas.

• • •

One of the hardest things a coach has to do is take the boredom out of training. Once players become bored, you're heading for a loss. You've got to try to give them a reason why they've got to win that next game, that it — not the game after or the game after that — is the most important thing.

• • •

It's up to you, the coach, to stick to the rules that have been set, whether they've been set by the players or by you. Players don't resent rules so much as a breakdown of authority or when coaches or administrators display favouritism in any way.

• • •

The responsibility of the coach goes past the football paddock. How his players conduct themselves when not under supervision is the yardstick.

• • •

A coach can influence people in the most minute ways. It isn't always what you say; it's what you do. If you deserve respect, you'll get it.

● ● ●

It takes a lot more time for a coach to prepare a team these days than it once did. The intelligence factor in the game has risen a hell of a lot. The time required to perform on match day has doubled. We have a more intelligent coach these days, who has to spend a lot more time at his job than ever before. The coach has to stick away his golf clubs for much of the winter these days. The skill of the player has improved, because the condition of the player, his stamina and endurance, has improved *(1987)*

● ● ●

How could I expect my staff, the officials, most importantly the players to maintain their poise under pressure if the head coach couldn't?

● ● ●

I like to think that my coaching didn't do too many of my players any harm. If they had the talent they had the opportunity.

● ● ●

In coaching, I know that I'm smarter now than I was last year, and smarter than I was in 1987, my last year as a club coach. But I know, too, that I haven't got the stamina to take it on again. I don't want to drive home from a losing game again. I've done that and it takes a lot out of you.

TWO

The Game

'The unpredictability of sport never lets you feel comfortable for too long.'

I think the beauty of sport is that there's no sympathy in it. While the game is on, you don't care if the bloke you're playing against has a defect; that's part of it. And when the match is over there are no excuses and all accolades go to the winner. That's how it should be. It's first or last, that's all.

• • •

When I first went to the USA in the late 1960s I knew what I was looking for — I wanted to find out how their coaches reacted to their game, because the principles of their game are exactly the same as ours. We're trying to catch the ball and put it up the other end. If you've got the football you've got to try to make some yards and if they've got the football you've got to stop them. Further, we we're all looking for the same sort of person, for someone who can play a game, catch the ball, stop the runner, and when they've got the ball they can pick up some yards.

Still, when I went, it wasn't as if I had a list of what I was looking for. But I was lucky enough to meet a man who became a close friend, Dick Nolan, who was for eight years (1968 to 1975) the coach of the San Francisco 49ers. I spent a tremendous amount of time with Dick, and those hours — and productive times with other people in the National Football League — reinforced a lot of ideas I already had. For example, they had determined that to be defensive player you actually needed more talent than the person who ran the football. I was pleased when I heard that, because I thought it was true; better than my instinct, they had stats to prove it. The explanation for it is that the man with the football reacts first, while the defensive player has to stop that runner. This means that the attacking player has the advantage, so the defensive player has to make up for that with talent and quickness. And he's got to be someone who wants to hit somebody.

The general philosophy in US football in the 1970s was that if your defence wasn't intact you couldn't win. The ball runner, he'd sell you season tickets, but the defensive player, he'd get you to the grand final (or, in their case, the Superbowl) and win it for you.

So I stayed with defence and I spent a long time working at it. Today, all the coaches in our league spend as much of their time on defence as I did. But back then I had an advantage because I practised defence and no one else did.

• • •

It's Sunday at your home ground, Cumberland Oval. Souths versus Parramatta. The game has been in progress for 25 minutes. The scoreboard reads: Visitors 16, Home team 2.

When you play 'coach', situations like this sure make it difficult to plan ahead.

Things that flash through your mind: I'll go straight home after the game; I'm not going to that dinner engagement my wife had planned; if some kid asks me for my autograph, I'll break his pencil.

You hear a voice in the crowd bellow out, calling us the 'Parramatta French' team. Large chunks of negativism infiltrate your mind.

Drop the captain ... the 'Bear' is too old ... and fat ... Price and Cronin need a spell ... the fullback should be playing halfback ... look at those second rowers, Beecher and Sharp, they're as dumb as two posts ... those club-footed wingers will die of cold is they don't get involved ... who in the hell let five-eighth Pattison leave this club ... three tries! ... our defence must be trying to play him into a Test match ...

That photographer taking my photo, why doesn't the dope watch the game? I wonder if he wants me to smile ...

I didn't have to coach, I could have been playing golf ... or fishing ...

Fourteen minutes to go in the first half, we cross for a try, Cronin converts. Scoreboard: 16–7 in arrears.

Four minutes left, we are in again, six behind as the hooter goes, ending the half.

In the sanctuary of the dressing room we check the players for possible injuries. Everybody's healthy ... well, that's something. We remind each other that we're not playing soccer, for if you are six behind in soccer you are playing without hope.

We hit the lead by a point with 19 minutes left. Now, you want the game to end. How slow the time moves. Before we reached the lead, the clock seemed to gallop; now it seems to have stopped.

Cronin scores a five-pointer under the posts. Parramatta is six in front. The game is out of reach for Souths. We win. I walk through the tunnel into our dressing room, trying to look intelligent and smoke-screening the fact that I've just given birth to a couple of ulcers.

You congratulate the players on a tremendous second half, knowing that they will never know what you were thinking of them early.

You remind yourself that when a team wins, you're not as smart as you would like people to believe. Or maybe as dumb when a team gets beaten. *(1981)*

'Kick to the seagulls.'

Jack Gibson to Peter Sterling. When asked for an explanation, Jack said,
'If there are seagulls there, there won't be players.'

> **'Well, they all seem to limp a little extra when they are replaced.'**
>
> Jack, after a player was replaced during the 1984 State of Origin series.

Finals are not that difficult to win — getting there is the tough part.

•••

After playing five games under the old 'unlimited tackle' rule, Arthur Beetson once said that the most encouraging aspect of the game was that the backs did not need to get their uniforms laundered after the game.

•••

Selectors are like referees ... no matter what decision they make, they can't please everyone.

•••

A sure way to help kill off our game is to have an all-in brawl or two in a game while playing on national television.

Many people who watch violence being committed feel it is OK. Witnessing rules being broken, blood being spilt by player on player, is 'entertainment'.

But when their kids are ready for team sports, they will select soccer or Australian football. They are parents who don't want to subject their kids to a game with unnecessary risk in a sport that can get out of control.

•••

The use of video evidence is not always conclusive, but it sure beats the memory bank of most witnesses.

•••

The game today is entirely different to when I played. But I still think it's pretty smart. Maybe the biggest change lies in the simple fact that if you're a bit slow today, mentally or physically, you're

NOSTRADAMUS JACK

In a newspaper column in July 1981, Jack Gibson proposed some rule changes for rugby league ...

On all tries, the conversion kick be taken in front of the goalposts on the 22-metre line

The introduction of kicking tees for goal shots

A total revision of the replacement rule

Scrap the five-metre rule in attack

The loose head and the feed be given to the attacking team in scrums

A far better contrast for uniforms when the club colours are similar — the visiting team has to change

A few weeks later, Jack was looking to the future once more ...

Rugby league has been the top winter game for players and spectators in New South Wales for 50 years. It has always commanded the biggest patronage, the best press coverage and more TV and radio time than rugby union, Australian football and soccer put together.

The situation will not automatically continue. For when you have good things happening to you over the years, you just go out there anticipating that's it's going to happen again.

That's tradition — but it's not good business administration.

When the entertainment starts to lose sales appeal, investigation usually focuses on several standard areas:

- Quality of the product
- Availability to the consumer
- Management control
- Presentation
- Price
- Marketing
- The rivals' product

not going to survive. And the size of the players — I was a prop forward, weighing in at 14 stone (89kg) and I was regarded as big. These days, I'd be a featherweight.

Players today have the luxury of a tremendous amount of time to get ready for a game. They train pretty much everyday. When we played, we trained two nights a week; everyone had to be there by 8 o'clock, and by then we'd all had our tea. It wasn't ideal, but it was the way it was then. Two nights a week, that was all … and an hour and a half was a long session.

• • •

The tackle part of today's game worries me these days. It's an arm wrestle and a leg wrestle and they won't let 'em play the ball. The aim now is to slow the game down, to not let the bloke with the ball get up and play it. There are three or four in the tackle, jumping on each other. I think the coaches encourage it and the referees and the rules let it happen. What goes on at the ruck definitely needs cleaning up. In my view that's the greatest need: to do something about the untidiness of the play the ball.

The scrums were a contest when I played, but not any more. Back then you quickly learned who to respect and who not to respect. But the rule changes of recent times have brought some good things. For example, that old thing of kicking at goal from scrum penalties wasn't too bright.

• • •

The runner will get a lot of fans in, but the defensive player will win grand finals for you. The defensive part of the game is the key. The runner has the football, he's going to make some yards and no one knows whether he's going to go right or left. The defensive player, on the other hand, has to read all that and then match the task through his own speed and strength. You can't put a value on the good defensive players.

• • •

Rugby league is a violent game, there's no other way about it. That's one of the things people go to see; they want to sit in the stand and feel and look at the violence as it happens. But the game is played with rules. What we've got to do with football is take out the unnecessary violence.

●●●

It wasn't my job to comment about how other teams played their football. The only thing that I ever went crook over was any coach who asked a player to foul an opponent. To me, coaches who do that must hate the game and hate the players, too. A coach is responsible not only for the players' conduct on the field, but off the field as well. If he encourages them to foul, that can easily go further than the football field.

AS QUEENSLAND AS RED CEDAR

In State of Origin's early days, there were many questions about just who was and who wasn't a Queenslander. This was Jack's take on the debate ...

The State of Origin match ... what qualifications are needed to make the squad?

Maybe a weekend holiday on the Gold Coast would be sufficient. I believe Mr and Mrs Cronin spent their honeymoon there, which could make Mick eligible.

John Ribot was born in France but played in Brisbane. He's OK.

Bob O'Reilly and Peter Sterling have been mentioned. Both were hatched in Queensland but left the nest at an early age. They're OK.

Steve Rogers played junior league on the Gold Coast for a season. That's nearly life member stuff.

My Dad and Mum had a red cedar saw mill in Atherton, Queensland, in 1910. That should make me at least eligible to be a spectator.

> **FIRST OR LAST**
>
> *Following the pre-season final in 1981, which Gibson's Parramatta lost to Eastern Suburbs, the Eels were criticised for not remaining on the field to see Easts presented with the winner's cheque and trophy. This is how Jack responded ...*
>
> At the game's conclusion, our players shook hands individually with the winners and then left for the sanctuary of the dressing room.
>
> In this game, you are either first or last.
>
> The rostrum is only for the winners. Competitors who have been in this situation know that if you have given your best and failed there is no point in staying ...
>
> The sportsmanship of a team is reflected by its actions on the field of play and Parramatta walked from the field as men. Competitors who have faced this situation will know what I'm talking about.

Sunday, September 27, Grand Final Day, the longest day of the year.

For the coach there is only tension, from the second you wake up until the final hooter that ends the drama.

The pressure comes on very strong, the last game where there is only one survivor. A 32-game season, 120 scheduled training sessions, compressed into one short afternoon. You win, you survive, there is nobody else to play.

Afterwards, the game, the season, is over ... and the win surpasses any sporting achievements that have come my way — my biggest thrill. I would like to be able to tape my emotions. I'll never forget the players and the staff for making it all happen.

I read a book once about an old coach. I have forgotten the contents, but will always remember the title: 'You Win With People'.

I do not know who to thank the most, but if a decision had to be made and I had to name the players, they would come from the men who had their name the longest — Edge, Cronin, Hilditch, Price and O'Reilly — and their women.

Maybe not so much for their unquestionable playing ability, but for their attitude, their confidence in themselves and the other players in the team.

Our welcome back at Parramatta Leagues Club was an experience that has had a tremendous impact on my wife and myself. The Sydney Cricket Ground scene was different; the audience was made up of winners and losers. At Cumberland, everybody was part of the four tries and four goals that gave Parramatta victory. The fans were great, they even left my car parking space vacant.

Winning, there is nothing like it — I can sure eat that stuff. *(1981)*

•••

'I see where rugby union is going professional. All that means is that they've decided to pay tax.' *(1995)*

•••

Rugby league doesn't create character ... it exposes it.

•••

'Rugby league' means when you don't play well you have no one to blame but yourself.

•••

Football games are not delayed by rain in the middle of the first or second half. That's always put me off summer. Furthermore, football umpires don't take the team off the field when the sun goes under a cloud.

•••

State of Origin rugby league matches prove that the meek don't inherit anything.

•••

The day that God invented rugby league he didn't do anything else but sit around and feel good.

THREE

Four Outstanding Teams

'The thing about the teams I had and won with is that I didn't stop them from winning.'

Easts 1967

My last year in grade football was 1964, with Wests. For '65, I followed Eastern Suburbs as a spectator, and went to quite a few of their games. The following year, I put in for the job as coach but they had an Englishman, a gent named Bert Holcroft, who got the job that year. Well, they didn't have much luck, didn't win a game, so the following year when I put in for the job again there weren't that many applicants. That made my task of getting appointed a lot easier.

From the start, I really worked on defence in 1967. And I wanted to take a little insurance out on the simple things. My attitude was that if we had the ball we had an opportunity, and if we kept it for as long as possible we'd get an advantage. We didn't want to pass up that advantage too easily. If we kicked it out, we didn't want to kick it out on the full. But mostly it was defence. I spent 50 per cent of my time on tackling practice — tubes and bags and anything I thought would benefit us. We lost our first three games and had a draw, and then won our next nine and ended up getting to the playoffs. Defence won it for us, because we only had 27 tries scored against us for the year.

First year I coached at Easts I received $1000. The next year, we had a tougher time but still had a better season. Yet when I put out my hand for the cheque they gave me $800. That didn't inspire me to stay. It didn't inspire me to leave either, but I did think the pay was a little light, so eventually I decided that for 1969 I'd just sit up in the stand.

> **'I don't think they were crook because [if you say that] you take something away from Queensland. I thought they played pretty strong, but Queensland was twice as strong.'**
>
> Jack, when asked by TV host Mike Gibson if New South Wales had been 'crook' in the opening State of Origin match of 1984. Queensland won 29–12.

St George 1971

After '69, I really wanted to get back into this coaching caper. I'd missed it. I got the job at St George because of one person, and one person only, and that was Norm Provan. If Norm hadn't been on my side I'd have had no chance of getting the position, but I did get it and we reached the final and the grand final in the two years I was there.

In 1971 we had all three grades in the grand final but we failed with the three of them. In first grade, we had an opportunity to win the football game. We were a point away with five or six minutes to go and we had opportunities, but we didn't score. We played well and we played strong, and if I'd known as much about coaching then as I know now, I think we might have won the football game. At least Souths, who won the game, were a championship side — we didn't get beaten by a team of mugs. And if Saints had won that game, maybe Souths could have said they were unlucky. I certainly never begrudged them their victory.

We were so close ... but close doesn't count in this game.

It's funny, I've been involved coaching in six grand finals, but if I'm asked which was the most memorable, the one that stands out is the loss I expected to win.

Easts 1975

We had a lot of talent. I couldn't add talent to them. It was my job to see that I didn't throw them out of gear, to protect that talent that they had and let them run with it.

The St George side we beat in the '75 Grand Final was a strong side. After all, they did get to the grand final. Yet we beat them 38-0. I've been on the receiving end of football games like that. In the first half we led 5-0, and at half time we were doing it as tough as Saints, but then in the second half the floodgates opened. This can happen in a football game and you've got no way of stopping it; we just kept coming at them and putting the ball over the line. But, as I said, I've been in other games when it's happened to me — when I've walked away and watched the video I've come to realise that we haven't played that bad, that our opponents just came and got us.

> **'There were no poor individual performances, but some played better than others.'**
>
> Jack on the 1984 Grand Final, won by Canterbury over Parramatta.

Parramatta 1981

For me, personally, winning the premiership with the Eels in 1981 was more of a relief than anything else. The year previously, they hadn't made the playoffs, so — at least as far as stress from other sources was concerned — there was a little bit of pressure off me: as the new coach, if I could get them into the playoffs it would've meant that I'd improved them a little bit. But we went all the way, against a lot of adversity. I had six or seven veterans in that team and to win a championship, I always felt that you needed a nucleus of at least six really tough, hard, seasoned veterans. I had that. You can't win it on youth alone.

We made Stephen Edge captain and in all my time, despite all the talent we had underneath him, we never thought about taking the captaincy off him. Yet he didn't play every Sunday, and if he was out we had a choice of who to pick instead. O'Reilly, Hilditch, Cronin, Price, Sterling ... that was the hard bit. You could have picked the alternative captain out of the hat.

The Parramatta premiership win that made the deepest impression on me was, without doubt, the first one. That whole town stopped. All those people who'd been cheering all those years, who'd been walking home saying, 'Maybe next year,' ... they didn't have to say that anymore. That's where my relief came from. I was happy that they no longer had to think that way. They'd been close, they'd had the talent, but they'd just missed out. And all of a sudden they'd won a championship.

A key to that win — to all three wins, 1981 to 1983 — was that throughout the players respected themselves and they respected everyone involved with the place. Respect is the thing. That's the prime thing: the player must respect the coach and his staff if they want to communicate and work towards a common endeavour. You must respect the coach. You don't have to like him, that's got nothing to do with it, it's not a popularity contest.

The players also appreciated the opportunity, without ever being satisfied with just being in the top grade. Further, we didn't want — and didn't have — the second grade players thinking, 'Geez, I'm happy to be in second grade.' We wanted them to be wanting to be up in that first team and we didn't want them believing that it was only selection bias that was keeping them out of the top team. We wanted them to have an ego; not to think that we were satisfied with them being second graders. This all said, on match day, you can only pick so many. There's always at least one tough selection decision to be made on match day.

We had quite a few of those in 1981.

FOUR

Talent is Secondary

'Attitudes are more important than rules.'

Not long after he became coach of the South Sydney Rabbitohs in 2003, Paul Langmack, asked what I would rate the single biggest asset a coach had to have. I told him 'trust'.

•••

It's the same answer in all occupations. Doesn't matter whether you're playing, coaching or working in a factory, you've really got to like what you're doing if you're going to work to your potential. You've got to like that stuff you're doing.

•••

Winning starts a long time before the gun goes off to start the game. I remember one season, people kept telling me that Mick Cronin was 'out of his slump'. Cronin had never been in a slump. You only had to look at his attitude through the week to discover that there were many ways in which he contributed to a win. Same with Edge, Price, Sterling, the team captains … they always started on the week previous to winning on Sunday. Their attitude to training, the way they dressed for training, they always had their gear right, they never looked to get a rub half way through training. That attitude is contagious. You've got to have it in a team.

• • •

I don't believe you can train 24 hours a day and become a good sportsperson if that's not your go. If you don't truly want to make it, you're never going to make the team. But if you've got some ability and you start to train and go the lengths necessary to succeed you will certainly improve. If I got a kid that started to improve, I kept him in that team all the time. Because — if he showed me a little improvement each Sunday — I didn't know where he was going to stop.

• • •

When a person is late or misses an appointment without a plausible explanation, you must consider that the meeting wasn't important enough to him. Not only is it a breach of contract, it shows a lack or respect for teammates, management and, most of all, him or herself.

Because you earn money out of a game doesn't make you a professional. The real pro always seems to have time to fulfil his or her commitments.

• • •

It's not who you play but how you play.

• • •

Talent is secondary to whether players are confident.

In 1987, after Jack retired as Cronulla coach, he was interviewed by the radio commentator Alan Jones. 'There are people who put stones in the road in competitive sport, aren't there?' Jones asked.
Jack's reply ...

'I feel you need them, they keep you awake.'

> Jones then continued: 'What about the people who have tried to put Gibbo away by putting stones in the middle of his road?'
>
> **'Well, if everyone's patting you on the back you go to sleep and then they're all laughing at you.'**

Sometimes I'd ask my players a question: 'Do you get frightened out there?' The ones that said no were the ones that *I'd* get nervous about. The ones who admitted they were fearful ... but went anyway ... they seemed to do better.

● ● ●

For success at anything, you've got to give it that little bit extra. The worst thing that can happen to anyone at any age, at any stage, is to look back over his or her shoulder and think: 'I could have done better.' To have a talent that is never used is a very sad legacy.

● ● ●

A coach should ask his players to make a commitment. I'd ask my players, 'What are you going to do for me?' To an individual: 'What are you prepared to do, if I start you?' And if they make a commitment and they don't even come close to it ... well, you've got to put somebody else in there. But if they try to do something about what they said they were going to do, you're obliged to support them.

● ● ●

A player who opens his mouth a lot isn't too confident. These type of players are trying to prop themselves up a little. The ones who talk a lot, who threaten a lot, who point the finger, you can bet your life they're doing it tough.

● ● ●

I go out and watch kids play golf all the time. Every so often, someone will say, 'Watch this bloke, he can play as good as Tiger

Woods, this bloke.' No risk, there's plenty who can play as good as a top pro, but their brain won't let them. There's always more pressure on the winner, but he can handle it.

● ● ●

I'm not an underdog man. I remember once hearing a member of parliament being asked what his tip was for the grand final. 'I'm tipping the underdog,' he says. 'We're the underdogs, so I'm going for the underdogs.' I thought, what a tragedy this politician is. I didn't mind him going for the opposition, but his reason for doing so was so hollow. It's tougher for the champion to stay on top.

● ● ●

Some people can take criticism in company and others can't. So you've got to be aware of each individual's problems. If a player is not playing well, he's looking to the coach for a little bit of consoling. He's got to find a friendly ear. We all need propping up sometimes and as the coach you've got to be ready to administer that. This player doesn't want to be loudmouthed out if he's made a blue. If he's a smart football player he'll be quite aware of his mistake; a coach should not only criticise them, but also tell them the answers. Get that right, and the player can take some assurance out of the fact that more than likely it's not going to happen again.

'The hardest part is when it's your turn to mag and there's nothing to say. I tend to keep my mouth shut unless I've got something to say. In this type of business you've got to pump something out. If you had time to think, you'd probably wouldn't say the same thing the second go.'

Jack on TV commentating.

If a kid has made some mistakes in the game, maybe cost the team a win, he's got to be able to come back and fight through that experience. If he's comes up with a fundamental mistake in the game, the coach doesn't want him to hide or start grabbing his leg and making out he's had a muscle pull or some damn thing. When one of my blokes made a mistake, we were looking for a positive reaction from that player. You can forgive a mistake. If it occurred while the player was trying to do something positive, that's one thing. But if a player was trying to do a negative thing, or nothing at all, or trying to hide, and he's come up with a mistake — that one's far harder to forgive than the other.

● ● ●

I was not going to cut anybody because they were down in one area or down in two. But if they were down in four or five areas, I was not going to use them because I didn't have the time. Before a player came to the club where I was coach, we certainly investigated whether he could contribute outside football. If he couldn't fulfil in that area, we weren't going to use him even though he could play. We'd tell a player, 'We can offer you this and that.' But it's got to be a mutual thing. I had to be convinced that the player was trying to make me successful and for me to get through to that player, he had to realise that I was giving him the opportunity to succeed.

● ● ●

If a player had a bad game and wouldn't admit it, I couldn't accept that. He's had a poor game, but thinks he's played well ... I put that player down as being just about uncoachable. I couldn't make room for him.

● ● ●

When you pick a team, you need to remember that each player has to have confidence in the people he's playing with. That's very important as far as the overall team effort is concerned.

● ● ●

When you criticise people, either as a group or individually, you need to be aware of how the to-be-criticised are likely to handle it. Maybe you start to tell them a few good things they've done and then bring up the mistakes they made. Always, if I was going to point out a mistake I needed to have worked out why the mistake had been made. It's not much good to me if I remind you that you've dropped the ball in a crucial situation unless I can tell you why you dropped it.

Some people can handle open criticism, plenty can't, but you don't wipe people out of the team because they can't handle it.

It's not a matter of not telling the more sensitive, or of being untruthful with them. That's the worst thing you can do. You just need to be clever about how you put them in the picture.

• • •

People look for praise and they expect it. And they like it best from the people they're most closely associated with.

• • •

Remember, someone had to be dropped for you when you were first promoted.

FIVE

Parents Have to Set the Example

'Small deeds beat grand intentions.'

I don't think I've ever read about the early and surprise retirement of any person connected with rugby league or sport who hasn't made 'the family commitment bit' the major reason for the retirement decision.

The only reason I was encouraged to stay coaching for so long by my family was they were frightened I'd stay at home if I quit.

•••

It's tough for young people today, really tough ... there are so many more temptations confronting them now than there used to be.

•••

Society has changed, but this hasn't: the parents have to set the example. They're the coaches. It might be Saturday morning and the kid has just played a game of football and got beat. With some parents, they're not happy with what the kid has done, and before he gets in the car he gets a smack on the backside and a rattle-up. It's a situation where the right type of coach can be a saviour. He won't smack the kid on the arse — he'll slap him on the back, with a few encouraging words: 'Hey kid, you can get better.'

It's a big thing, giving recognition to players. You don't have to be five years old or 15 years old or 55 years old to appreciate some encouragement, maybe a few positive words after things haven't gone so well. We're all in the market for that, for some appreciation.

•••

I was down watching some kids' water polo not so long back and the coach was screaming and carrying on. And there was a bloke over the other side of the pool, one of the parents, who listened to all this noise for a while and then called across to the coach: 'Do you want me to get a gun?'

He'd had enough of this bloke pounding and pounding away at the kids. With coaches like that, it seems as if that is all they've got. And where do they go from there? If the team doesn't react to the rattle-up, what can possibly work? These sort of coaches never hold back an idea, they've just got to get it out of their mouths. Generally, they're trying to coach the parents or to impress the parents.

Say you've got a coach with some kids and the coach is all right; he or she is low profile and appreciates the kids, is not mouthing off and overcoaching. The parents will watch that coach ... and they'll do the same. But if you've got a loudmouthed coach running up and down the sideline, then that behaviour encourages the parents and next minute there'll be 20 of them tailing along behind the coach.

Many young people in gaol never had the opportunity to play football or a contact sport. Football can offer so much. But if a kid gets overcoached by the parents, if he gets forced to do things, the first opportunity that comes along when he can make up his own mind, he'll leave the sport. He doesn't want to put himself in that situation ever again, it's too embarrassing, too tough for him.

I firmly believe there's too much emphasis in the pre-adolescent on the win situation, rather than on the pleasure of being able to compete.

The coach is a great influence on the families of those involved with the team. I believe the first job of a coach is to coach the family and let the kids look after themselves. A coach who can do that is going to be successful.

•••

I think the kid must find some solace in the coach. If a boy has had a poor game, the coach has to be able to put his arm around the kid and say, 'Hey, don't let it bug you, you worked away, you've done a lot of good things there.' Pick out the pluses.

•••

All kids can do is the best they can, to play to their potential. I couldn't give a footballer a higher accolade than saying to him, 'You've played your best, done your best.' There's nothing after that, is there? You can't say you played beyond your best. When someone plays their best, they've reached a new level.

COACHING IS TEACHING

I've been in rugby league all my life, but I didn't care what sport my children played and I don't care what sport other parents' children play. What does concern me are the philosophies and principles of the coach. That is my only concern.

I don't want some dope coach selling kids the story that if you don't physically intimidate your opponents you can't be a winner. And that you have to claw, scratch, kick and spit your way to victory.

Coaches who use the personnel at their disposal for this type of approach are guilty of manslaughter. Rugby league must be a game where the non-aggressive person can still feel comfortable.

Coaching is teaching. If the coach can simplify the game, a player may turn into the tiger he is supposed to be.

The crucial area with children is fear. Some kids are fearful of body contact. That is when the coach has to explain that it is quite normal to have fear ... and that everyone has a fear — be it cats, heights, snakes or whatever. Any time a kid shows a sign of toughness — no matter how small it may be — that has to be recognised. Any time he backs off through fear ... well, you don't mention it. Or you tell him you'd be frightened, too.

SIX

Motivation Comes From Within

'The secret to getting ahead is getting started.'

If you enter the dressing room immediately before a game you see a lot. In my day, some players would lie down, someone would do some push-ups or body presses, someone would do this, someone would do that. Each had his own method of motivating himself before the game began.

Right before the game, in the last 10 minutes, it's the players themselves who've got to work at being motivated right. At this late stage, you can't show them a film to get them focused. Players can't get motivated by a five-minute speech from someone else just before they run out onto the paddock. When the contest starts, it's certainly not about what the coach said a minute ago.

Once you get out there you're worrying about survival. All I told my players was that you survive yourself. I didn't want them worrying about any team situation. It's you, it's up to you to be the best player you're capable of, to get the job done. It's my job, the coach's job, to worry about the football team. If the player can fulfil his own ego out there; if he can come off, be realistic and honest, and know that he's had a good football game, then he's one man who's helped the team as a whole.

I worry when footballers aren't nervous before big games. If they're not nervous, they're not afraid and they're not worried about the problems they've got to face in a few minutes' time, they're kidding themselves. Sure, they're *outwardly* confident, but they're not the confident people a lot of people think they are. They're the ones who seldom produce.

•••

To me, the word 'motivator' means, 'Can he win with the talent at his disposal?'

Motivation comes from within. I feel that if I'm motivated by desire and have confidence in my team, their ability to perform is sufficient.

You can't motivate a post and all teams have their share of logs.

•••

If you train hard and think right, you can be as good as you want to be.

•••

In football, if you're standing still, you're going backwards fast.

A FEW WORDS ON LEADERSHIP

A good captain is essential for a team to survive in the rugged world of rugby league. One of the main ingredients of winning is your on-field leader.

The leadership qualities of a footballer, or anybody else for that matter, are assessed on his reaction under pressure. He must have the ability to submerge his ego for the benefit of the team. He must be positive, not negative.

Whatever play a captain calls, the team must react positively to that call, even though it may be the wrong play for that situation.

In the early 1980s, the big play seemed to be for teams to watch motivational films or tapes before a game. Coaches were looking for that little bit more, that winning edge, hoping that an inspirational movie would tap some unused power in the players. Someone would say after a big win, 'We showed the boys *Rocky IV* before the match and they played like champions.'

I always wanted to find out what cartoons the losers had been watching. I never wanted to show those shows to a team I was coaching.

• • •

A good coach doesn't pick out the negatives, he focuses on the positives. All a player wants to hear in the few minutes of halftime is what it is that might make him a better player. You don't worry about the scoreboard; the scoreboard is for the people in the stands. You worry about the answers and sometimes that can just be to pat the player on the back and say, 'You'll be OK, kid.'

SEVEN

Coach Killers and Other Players

'The only way you can find out if blokes can play is to get them to meet talent head on.'

Good players will be good under old rules and new rules. Just the same, rule changes don't make good players bad ones or bad players good ones.

• • •

There are some players you can definitely win with and others you can't. Some players always leave the impression that they will have an exceptional game *next* week. They call them 'coach killers' — they are everybody's pick to start in games but you never win with them.

• • •

I'm dead set against players not working. They've got to be productive. I've said many times that you can't hang around being a bonehead all week and come out on Sunday and show everyone how smart you are. You're much more likely to show how *dumb* you are. Coaches are probably getting smarter at keeping their players occupied now — but there's still a lot of idle time to fill in. What do they do? Go and watch a video? Have a bet on a horse? You can't train all day. As far as I'm concerned, they've got to have a job — something to give them purpose, and something to get them ready for the reality of life after football.

The thing is, they can't be playing football at 36. It's over by then, but as far as life is concerned there's still a long way to go. In my time as a coach the question of spare time wasn't even discussed, because everyone worked. Even today, in my view that's the way it should be — you've got to have a job. The game itself won't hold you together. And remember, for some players it all finishes very early.

• • •

My definition of a gifted athlete is one who, in the tension of the game, when the scores are locked close together, is going to do something. He's not the person who will put on another couple of tries for you when you're winning by 20 or 30.

• • •

When a coach assesses a player's value, one question he should always ask himself is: 'Can this individual make my life as a coach a little easier?'

• • •

I'd hate to get wounded like a soccer player … you'd be in bad shape! They roll over, screech, point the finger, take 10 deep breaths and then they're miraculously back up and playing again. But one of the attractions of soccer is that they don't feed them water endlessly like they do league players and union players. I'm only half joking here. In rugby league we've got three blokes taking water out so often that some of them seem to be camped out there permanently.

I went down to watch the Southern Districts rugby union side play one day. Before they went out, I was asked if I could say something to the players. And I said to them, 'Can you give me at least a bit of time today during the breaks in play when you *don't* have a drink of water?'

The only person who objected was their doctor, who was worried about them drying out or something. What I was really doing was suggesting to them that they should leave the water boys where they were and think a bit more about something positive ... like the football match.

Well, they kicked off and after a couple of short runs, one of their blokes kicked a field goal. They'd been out there about three minutes. Four of them went straight for the water bottle. I'm thinking, I might get them a camel. I don't agree with all the interference that goes on out on the field, all the advice that is handed out by the runners. The coaches give their players jobs to do and the players don't need to be overloaded ... with water or information.

• • •

The coach gets a kick from getting a player who had showed no real ability but, while you've been with him, he's risen. You're a part of that, you're a part of his success and you get this feeling ... hey, I helped that bloke succeed a little. Probably works in reverse, too. If you get a good player, you're working together for some time and he starts to decline, you think, 'I might have been in that.'

• • •

The life of a football coach has many highs and lows. When the team wins the coach is not as smart as he is often made out to be, nor is he as dumb as he may appear when the team loses.

The most difficult or unpleasant time in coaching seems to be when personal confrontation with the player is necessary — such as when you have to tell an individual that you can't use him for this game or for the season. In 1981, my first year at Parramatta, I had decided to let go two athletes with fine records, Lew Platz and Mark Levy. I could not see them playing first grade in the near future, because of the younger talent I had at my disposal.

Such decisions have to be made, but are extremely difficult when the players concerned have been outstanding club men.

> **'Players should realise that they are in this game for one common endeavour. To make them all richer — money and character-wise. Trying to put each other out of the game should not be their game.'**
>
> Jack commentating after a brawl in a State of Origin match, 1984.

If they've got a brain you've got a chance. But they've got to be able to use the brains they have. Big brains, little brains, as long as they've got some, and they're using them, that's all that's required.

• • •

I never believed in putting on a 'crash' training session or an extra one, unless I'd given the players at least a week's notice. They've got to plan their lives, and my job was to tell them what we'd be trying to do on Sunday and ask for them to report on time.

The ones that are bored with training are not really going to make it, they're cup of tea players, in and out of the joint within a season.

In one sense, I used to value a player like a car — there are only so many miles in it. You used to see blokes playing a full season in Sydney and then going to England to play in the off-season. That was a lot of football games, and it was going to take a year off their careers further down the line. But I do concede that some footballers have a longer life expectancy than others.

• • •

A club must have players who can handle pressure, no matter what their grade. You can't always buy those types, but you have to find them to succeed.

• • •

The dirty footballer becomes a timid man at the finish, looking for somebody who's going to have a go at him. His behaviour usually reflects a loss of concentration on the job at hand. If he's thinking about pointing the finger or singing out, 'I'll nail you, No. 12', he's become an individual in a team game and pretty useless as far as what we're trying to accomplish. It's a violent game, so you must have control of yourself when you participate in it. Indeed, the time you really need control is when things are going against you. Anybody can let one go, but it's always a sign of weakness.

• • •

I've seen plenty of 'brilliant' players running around who can come off after a game and the public will think he's had a pretty good game. But he hasn't contributed to the overall team effort, he's only looked after his own game. These players pace their games.

I always wanted my blokes to think that they must do things in twos. They must do two tackles together or be prepared to do two runs together. If you could get your team members to do things in threes no one would ever beat you. But I found that it was the hardest thing to get a footballer who had just made a 20-metre run to prepare immediately to go again — that's the time, when they haven't got the ball, that's when we needed them to stay in the game. Too many players who make a 20-metre run think they've got a licence to throw that ball anywhere or to stand around thinking that their run wasn't too bad.

'I have no long-range plans about the future years — only the present. The goal will be our next game and our next performance ...'

'What luck is needed to succeed, we'll try to put ourselves in a position to receive some, when it's jumping around.'

'I won't be going along with the old football cliché — "let the ball do the work". We'll be using bodies.'

'I don't want players with talent alone — only the ones that are prepared to work.'

Some comments from Jack after being appointed coach of Cronulla for 1985.

I could accept a player making a mistake. It depended on the circumstances, and more importantly whether he was working at it. He must be doing something about it. If he had a bad penalty rate but was doing something about it, I could accept his mistakes, but if he was doing nothing about it I just couldn't use him. He might have suited other coaches, but he didn't suit me.

• • •

The senior player needs as much coaching as the rookie. In fact, he expects it. Just because he's been around for a few years doesn't mean that he still doesn't want to go on learning about the game.

• • •

The modern player is more intelligent, better conditioned, he's got stronger discipline and he's more community minded, compared to those of past eras. And it's a rare football player whose mouth doesn't contain his own teeth these days.

• • •

At the start of one season, I addressed the players this way: 'Bring along your scrapbooks next week for the barbecue, we need some fuel. Past successes won't count ... it's what you do this year.'

• • •

When it came to players being late for training, any excuse I hadn't heard before, I accepted.

• • •

One of the main reasons I think rugby league is best game of them all is the players and the fact that when they're out there with a number on their back there is nowhere for them to hide.

• • •

The great ones are humble, they're easy to be around.

EIGHT

A Team Sport

'Teamwork will always beat individual brilliance.'

The general public, when looking at a team running onto the field, only considers the players and the coach. But the back-up needed to keep a team healthy and in the right frame of mind is so easily passed over.

A rugby league team can be compared to a jumbo jet — it takes only a couple of pilots to keep the plane in the air but they wouldn't become airborne without a groundstaff many times their own number.

• • •

One season, a boy offered an excuse I hadn't heard before when I asked why he had missed the training session.

'Oh, my sister had a baby,' he said.

I didn't know whether he helped with the delivery, but I gave him the rest of the season off to look after it.

• • •

It's no secret that rugby league — perhaps more than any other game — is a team sport. Yet how well the gears of a football machine mesh is decided by the individual efforts and achievements of each team member.

> **Who is Parramatta's most valuable player? I've been asked that question many times and the answer I give has changed just as many times. After each game you consider the person who has been most inspirational in a team effort ... *(1981)***

Dr Bill 'Swing' Buckingham served as the Eastern Suburbs doctor from 1958 to 1982. When I was at the club he was always there when I needed propping up with encouragement after poor games when playing, or losing games when coaching.

On one occasion, I asked Dr Bill to look at the cut eye on one of our back-row forwards at halftime. Just as the team was about to return to the field, I asked if this player could continue.

The reply was definite: 'No chance, the injury is too severe.' I put on a replacement.

When we returned to our seats I told Bill that I hadn't realised the injury was that bad.

'It wasn't,' he replied. 'But he hadn't made a tackle and I couldn't bear to watch him for the rest of the match.'

•••

Often, the reason given for a team missing the playoffs is 'injuries'. But more often than not the major injuries to a football team are inflicted when internally the club cannot master the small problems that inevitably appear during a season.

Successful clubs seem to have the healthy competitors, whether they be players or administrators ...

•••

I think team sport is a must for young people. There's got to be some attraction in life apart from homework. The experience of playing a team sport — even if that career is a short one — will stay with you and there'll be benefits for the working career ahead.

> **'They get cut. And they should realise that they have cut themselves; no one else did it.'**
>
> Jack in the early 1980s, when asked what happens to players who don't follow his 'rules'.

You don't appreciate it if it comes easy. You can see what happens with individuals who pull together as a team until they reach a pinnacle or accomplish their objective. Then they start to fade ...

• • •

In rugby league, there is no place for a selfish player, irrespective of his ability.

NINE

The Front Office

'Too many people are ready to carry the stool when a piano is to be moved.'

To have the front office right is the *whole* thing in football. If you haven't got that, your football team will crumble away. Nothing surer.

• • •

To win the championship, you need people of quality — on and off the field. During my time as coach, I had the support of great examples of those sorts of people in Mick Souter (team conditioner) and Alf Richards (ambulanceman/trainer). They were the best in the business and their advice was valued and used throughout the time we were together.

'There must be a break between meals to enjoy the food.'

Jack on the early weeks of the 1984 season, when eight complete rounds were played in the first five weeks.

You sometimes see the wrong people getting appointed to jobs at different places. On many of these occasions you know from their previous form or their background that they're not right for the job and they're never going to be. I've seen it with coaches and I've seen it with players over the years. And it's just about always the case that there's someone at the joint who reckons they can turn them around, turn them into Dudley Do-Rights. But they never can. I could quote an example or two in football right now.

●●●

If you want to slaughter a good idea, hand it over to a committee; they'll really punch a few holes in it. Everyone talks about the players, but there's got to be some quality control in management. That's the first thing.

●●●

In my first year at Parramatta, we won a couple of games and then lost three in a row. The management committee asked me to come in and have a talk. I had my back up a little bit, because I thought, 'Hello, they've got a problem with my coaching methods.' But it wasn't that at all. Instead, they said, 'Jack, we don't think we've got the players to survive and we suggest we try to refurnish in a few areas.' When the chips were down they showed they had faith in me. That meant a lot.

●●●

Everybody has ideas on what's good and bad for the game. Some like to go back in time and tell you that rugby league was better and more competitive then. But in most cases, reliving the old days was more pleasant than living them.

I remember one established club decision-maker got some press when he said, 'There is too much defence in the game. It's killing it as a spectacle.'

He might have had something there. When I was coaching, I often wondered what my blokes could do other than defend when we weren't in possession of the ball.

●●●

The rise and fall of the game depends on how smart the people in the front office are. Trouble is, it still seems to me that it isn't too difficult for a person to get into a position in a football club where he makes decisions on where millions of dollars go. Sometimes these people have no experience of handling money and have never paid a person's wage out of their own pocket.

It's like government. Someone who was once in local government gets given a portfolio. Suddenly they're the boss and are making decisions about things they know nothing about.

Salary caps are put in place to stop untalented administrators sending clubs broke.

The only people who are selected on merit in clubs are the teams. Their performances are assessed every weekend. The administrators bypass that, which is why they can get away with not being talented.

• • •

A player has been there for a long time, but now he's been dropped. In his place, a young bloke has made the team for the first time. But in the papers, it'll be the demotion that gets the headlines, with the promotion underneath in small print. Too often, they work on the negatives more than the positives. To me the headline should have been young bloke makes first grade, replacing veteran, but they don't work like that. Bad news gets all the ink.

• • •

I never think there should be a restriction on the truth. That applies to life, it applies to rugby league. If a coach points out that a referee made a blatant mistake and it's a proven fact that he did, then the League should run with that. If the coach is wrong, then fine him. We have to protect the referee. He needs protection; but if he's made a mistake he's going to learn a lot quicker if he's accountable for the error. For the coach to say something that's true, and the whole story is on video for everyone to see, and for the League to then fine him for pointing it out, that's wrong.

Not for the first time in the game's history, people are starting to think that the man in the middle's performance is deteriorating a little. It's not that at all — it's just that the coverage today is that much better and we can pick his mistakes that much quicker and clearer.

•••

To me, today's league referees are getting over-coached, and loaded up with advice. One thing they should shoot out straight away is that electronic hook-up they stick in their ears. That is only putting more pressure on the referee. He's trying to wrestle with that while adjudicating on what he's seen with his own eyes.

Refereeing decisions can be (and have been) the difference between the winning and losing of games. The first thing that's got to be done for the refs is that their workload has got to be lightened. I don't know how they concentrate at all with blokes chattering in their ear. If the referees are not confused most of the time ... well, they should be.

I do like the use of the video in try decisions. Sure, it eats up a bit of time, but these days they make their decisions pretty quickly.

•••

The referees' workload should be the prime factor when rule changes are considered. Rule changes which place more pressure on the referee only lead to more controversy.

•••

Super League hurt the game tremendously. It was only the quality of the sport that got it through. It brought total inflation into the game, which now is going to be there forever and a day. Super League busted country football, really blew holes in the game in the bush. Look at a joint that was once strictly rugby league — St Gregory's College at Campbelltown, south-west of Sydney. What the split in football did to them is that *they've* still got players, but there aren't the teams any more who will come up and play them. St Gregory's have five or six teams, maybe more, and they want to give them a game every week, but these days they can only find a couple of opponents. The tragedy of the whole Super League thing was that virtually none of the money that was spent went back into the game. It went into buying cars, into buying real estate, into punting ... and into the pockets of the players' managers.

• • •

I was once asked how much footballers should be paid, and I replied, 'Players are paid the going rate, they don't set the fees. Officials do that.'

In my view, we should never bag the players for the money they receive from playing the game. It's only been given to them by the people they work for. As professionals, they're expected to do the best deal they can for themselves. So they've had nothing to do with the spiralling costs of the game (which certainly seems to me to be getting out of hand).

• • •

People like to say that players have no loyalty to their clubs, but that's not their fault. Most times, they don't want to leave the club. In my experience, there were very few instances of a player who's had a little success with a club who wanted to go elsewhere. But then other clubs come in and offer them so much money they've got to reconsider, after they learn that their 'home' club can't compete with that type of bread. I doubt it's changed now. Practically every player I know plays for less money for his club than he could get from somewhere else, so I never blame the player on this issue.

TEN

Fans

'A good football game can add flavour
to a hot dog.'

If participants in a sport are risking a fatal injury while they 'play', then there's a lot of attraction for spectators. If they'd offered front-row seats to the Iraq war they would have filled the joint. That's the nature of the beast.

• • •

First and foremost, the fans wants to see their team win. Second, they want to see a game that features some skill. They also want to see their team play the game and play it tough. They'll accept a loss under those circumstances, but if they go and watch their team throw the towel in a little bit, they feel embarrassed.

• • •

When I was with Parramatta, someone told me that at the workplace of our sponsor, James Hardie, when Parramatta won, very seldom would they have anybody off on the following Monday. They all turned up, they all wanted to shake hands with each other and share that winning feeling. But when they we got beat there were a lot of absentees.

TO THE FANS

Jack's ode to the followers of Eastern Suburbs ...

Hey Roosters!
Do we play this game for company?
(It's a novel way to meet)
Do we play this game in winter
to generate some heat?
Do we play this game for victory
Or are we happy in defeat?
Or is it just for profit...
Or to think that we're elite?

(Chorus)

To our fans we tell you
If you have not been told
We play this game for all of us
We play it from the soul!

We'll send you home without a moan
When victory comes our way,
But knowing in advance
That it never comes to stay.
We'll remember strong when things went wrong
You never walked away...
Standing out there in the cold.
So, please join with us and say:

(Chorus)

To our fans we tell you
If you have not been told
We play this game for all of us
We play it from the soul! *(2002)*

•••

For many people, their football team is the only thing they've got to cheer about. We don't want to say that, but it's a fact. That team's success is what's going to make them a winner, it's their life. When their football team gets beat they want to hide in the cupboard.

•••

It's a simple equation, and the league should never lose sight of it … forget about the fan and he or she will forget about attending.

•••

The comfort of watching sport on television with the push of a finger is temptation No. 1 for non-attendance.

SOME GIBSON 'ONE-LINERS'

'Usually the one you play.' — *when asked what was the team to beat.*

'Not when you lose.' — *when asked whether playing at 'home' helps.*

'They said that about the lions and the Christians.' — *when told that rugby league was 'only a game'.*

'What about the rest of the week?' — *after being wished 'good luck on the weekend'.*

'We only did one thing wrong … lose.' — *when asked, 'What went wrong?'*

ELEVEN

Facts of Life

'Mistakes made in the past must not be repeated.'

There are plenty of feuds around in rugby league today — invariably involving people who have grossly over-inflated views of their own importance in the game. Because they are the way they are, they have no way of getting out of the blues they find themselves in. The egos get in the way.

• • •

If you want to get married, you have to want to 100 per cent. Don't gamble on it. If there's one per cent doubt, don't do it. It's like buying a house — the main thing to evaluate is whether you like it.

• • •

Most people would like to censor criticism when it's pointed in their direction, but have no restrictions on flattery. We have no trouble digesting those pats on the back. We can sure eat that stuff up.

About 90 per cent of all media reports on the game of rugby league, players and officials are of a positive and praiseworthy nature. When the game or the administration is criticised it is usually done because the author or commentator considers the criticism warranted and is genuinely concerned about the game's survival.

Sometimes it is unfounded, sometimes it is constructive. Does this game of ours expect flattery or need it all the time?

An old gent, when asked to give his parallels on flattery and criticism, said: 'Flattery will send you to sleep and criticism will keep you awake. So, you see, we all need a fair share of each.'

• • •

What it takes to become a man often surfaces in the simplest ways.

• • •

When it comes to credibility, in my opinion there is no halfway house. It's like enthusiasm — you are either enthusiastic or you're not. With credibility, you either have it or you don't.

• • •

I'll never apologise for not being something else.

• • •

I went to the Veteran Boxers' Association reunion a couple of times — and I was very, very impressed. The old fighters all had something to say, and they all saluted each other. There was a lot of respect there. They had shared the experience of a tough sport — probably the toughest sport — and they appreciated each other. There was a genuineness about the handshakes and the greetings. The mateship was very strong.

You can't kid once you get into that ring. I spent 17 years going down to the fights at the old Sydney Stadium. Some of the blokes back then never trained at all. They'd just get a week's notice on a fight ... and turn up. Bronco Johnson, who was a colourful Queensland middleweight in the 1950s, was one of my favourites. He was an entertainer, all action. I liked Rocky Gattellari too. He'd always give the fans their money's worth. He was a real people's person was Rocky; he'd never forget a name and his hand would be out there ready to shake yours. Before he fought Burruni for the world title in Sydney his connections took him up to Lithgow and hid him away up there. It just drained the energy out of him. He was gone before he got into the ring.

• • •

When the gambling bug gets a hold on someone you can probably say it's right up there shaking hands with drugs in terms of the amount of control it has over a person. For employers, there's a simple message — you don't employ people who take drugs and you don't employ people who are gamblers. In both cases, they'll finish up using your money.

AN EXPENSIVE LESSON

When Neville Charlton came to Eastern Suburbs from Western Suburbs in 1962 it was the first year that the Easts club had the hotel at Bondi Junction which effectively acted as the licensed or 'leagues' club. The leagues club donated £1000 pounds to the football club and they spent £600 of it buying Charlton. The only other bloke who got money out of that was my fellow front-rower Terry Fearnley, who got £400. That took care of the thousand. So I went over to Newtown and I told them I was interested in playing there — and they were interested, too.

They gave me £500 to join them for the season. That was on a Friday night, so I shook hands with them and signed the contract. On the Saturday night my wife Jude and I went across to the Newtown club, but we couldn't get in because there was some rule that visitors couldn't get in until 8 o'clock. So we went up the Cross instead, for a Chinese feed. After that, I went down to the 'Game' — Perc Galea's illegal gambling club at the top of Kings Cross — bit the house for 500 ... and did the lot on baccarat! Actually, I had 60 or 70 quid in my kick ... so I did a bit more than 500. That was my pay for the year with Newtown. Gone!

The only good thing to come out of the experience was that I learned from it. This was a one-off; I came away from the experience bruised but a little wiser. I didn't chase the lost '500' and I never let the punt beat me like that again.

Gambling is a disease ... when the flea jumps on your back and gives you a little bite it's got the potential to strip you of everything you have. Yeah, I was a gambler ... I gambled a lot ... but I hated losing, probably more than I liked winning, and that was my saviour. I wanted to gamble and win, but I sure didn't want to gamble and lose. And the strength of that distinction was enough to keep me out of it.

It doesn't leave anyone alone once it gets a grip. When I worked at Thomas's — Thommo's Two-Up Game — for 12 years, I'd see blokes who first of all came in dressed in suits, and really looking the part. Two or three weeks later, they might come in looking not quite as sharp. And you'd see them decline quite quickly. Before long, they'd be standing out the back, in the place we used to call the 'loose box' — for the brokes. They no longer had anything to bet with. When it gets to that stage, people will pawn anything, and they don't care who they bite. The temptation becomes too big for them and they can't resist going back. Gambling's hold on many people is so savage that they simply can't get up and walk away from it.

If you can have a bet and walk away ... well, you haven't got a problem. But if you've got to stay there, just can't walk away, you've got a problem all right. It's not easy to beat, and you probably won't beat it on your own.

Nowadays, the country has just about been killed by all the poker machines and the different opportunities to bet that are offered to people. It's the No. 1 way that we're going down the spout as a nation. Governments think that it's a solution — pulling all the money that they do out of the gambling racket — but it's no solution for society.

• • •

People running sport have an obligation to try to stop the use of performance-enhancing drugs. I think they've done fairly well in rugby league, putting in place a policing system that's fairly effective. It's a reality of professional sport now that some players will do *anything* that might help them, irrespective of what it might do to their health.

• • •

Drugs in the wider sense shorten everything up. They reduce your ability to make decisions, they reduce your livelihood ... and ultimately your life. When performance-enhancing drug-taking first started in sport at least you could say that the people involved had no education, no idea of what the drugs were doing to them. But now we know ...

• • •

In Australia, drugs remain our No. 1 industry, our No. 1 killer. It's just a jungle there, it's open go. It's as easy to buy a hamburger as it is to buy drugs. What astounds me is that for many, drug-taking is so 'normal' that they ask *me*, 'What's the matter with you? Where've you been for the last 30 years?'

Everyone's looking for a solution, but you can't turn to page 64 of a coaching manual and find out what to do if you find yourself in a situation where your kids are doing drugs. But realise this: before your girl or boy is 12 years old they're going to come into contact with drugs, come into contact *directly* with drugs; their mates are going to have them, they're going to be offered them, they're going to be taking them.

We've got to come up with a game plan, some coaching, so that when this thing does strike, parents and children will have some knowledge about how to handle this situation. It's a tragedy. Can you imagine a 10-year-old or 12-year-old kid making a decision on that?

One thing I do know is that frightening kids won't work. You don't get results if you try to motivate by fear. That doesn't get anywhere, especially with addicts, because they don't give a shit any more that they're doing it. You can't risk your life if you haven't got one.

And on the other side, when many people read that somebody has died of an overdose their reaction is: 'There's another bad one dead.' In their view, they couldn't have been a good person because as far as they're concerned good people don't take drugs. If a man or a woman, boy or a girl, has died of a drug overdose they must have been a thief, or worse, so that death is 'not so bad'.

But most likely that overdose victim wasn't always bad. And it is still someone's child, someone's brother or sister. Someone owns that body. Somebody has got to bury that body. There'll be too much burying before we've worked this thing out.

●●●

The coach must realise what a tremendous responsibility he carries. He might be the difference between a person spending time in the 'Peter' (prison) or doing something worthwhile with his or her life.

●●●

A coach can influence people in the most minute ways. It isn't always what you say; it's what you do. If you deserve respect, you'll get it.

TWELVE

Nowhere to Hide

'The toughest lesson to learn is probably the one you thought you had already learned.'

To win anything you've got to have a toughness about you. The team's got to be tough, that infiltrates into individuals, and then you've got to have a tough leader. At Easts in 1967 we had a great kid called Jimmy Matthews, who was captain at the time because he played to his ability every Sunday. People liked to play with him. He was efficient. He could get the job done, make few mistakes, he had quickness, an excellent goalkicker, an athlete.

•••

I looked for a positive reaction from the player whose cubby house fell down during a game. You can't win with players who make mistakes then go and hide until the time is right to get back in the action.

•••

The only players I knew who rejected the significance of a tackle count were the individuals who hid in defence and left the tough part of the game to their teammates.

•••

At times I used to stand near where the players ran onto the field before the game and at halftime, and listen to the predictions of some opposing teams as they walked or sometimes ran onto the field.

In all cases, the players who make the most noise are the individuals who threaten verbally about how they are going to exterminate their opposition — but they never seem to actually do it. They only manage to embarrass the tough competitors in their teams.

The player or the boy who makes all the commotion on the way to the field is only drawing attention to himself, hoping that somebody will think that he plays without fear. But in reality he's crying out for help.

• • •

You'd like to think the preparation for a grand final is done well before the game. A grand final is about 12 months' preparation. The toughest part is not winning it, but getting there.

• • •

A tough football team should radiate its character to the extent that playing them would be like taking a walk on a dark night on the wrong side of Kings Cross ...

You're not sure you're going to get bowled over, but you're not sure you're not either.

• • •

There's a huge difference between a tough player and a dirty player. The game offers the opportunity for players to show their toughness, and it takes a much tougher individual to play with the rules they're given rather than cheap shot somebody. What happens to dirty players is that they eventually finish up chickening out themselves.

When a player starts punching, he's showing that he's immature, insecure, even frightened. Once a player gets personal, he's forgetting about the job at hand. He shouldn't be proving something to the other player or the crowd. He should be proving to himself that he has control.

In many instances he will have to submerge his ego.

THIRTEEN

Heroes

'If you want to destroy society,
talk down the heroes.'

Before I write about the great ones, a few words on Jack Gibson the footballer. The only thing I regret about me as a player is that I did have a tendency to look back over my shoulder. I could have been a better player than what I produced. I regret that I never gave it the time that I should have.

That was me. If I'd coached myself in those days I'd have been … well, that's a tough one … I wasn't that easy to get through to.

Brian Clay

One bloke who I know for sure I didn't relish playing against was St George's renowned five-eighth Brian 'Poppa' Clay. If I was on one side of the ruck and he was on that same side, I'd get to the other side. I played a lot better without him hanging around. He was pretty close to the perfect example of the effective defensive player. He'd never mouth off and forget the game, or hit someone in the mouth with a fist. He had all the attractions as a player, and off the field he had the personality to go with it. Seven days a week.

> The third of final Test of the 1984 Australia–Great Britain Test series is finally over, and up in the commentary box, the Channel Nine team are having a hell of a job wrapping up their telecast. Ian Maurice has one last question to ask of Nine's expert, Jack Gibson, but a technical problem cuts in before Jack can give his reply. Maurice tries again, wanting to know what Jack's favourite moment from the series was, but again the gremlins take over and Jack's reply is stifled. Take three, and again Jack is silenced. Take four ...
>
> ### *Ian Maurice:* 'Well, Jack, the series is over. What's the highlight to your mind?'
>
> ### *Jack Gibson:* 'Well, Ian, I haven't thought about it much ...'

Barry 'Bunny' Reilly

I remember a bloke I had at Easts. He got into a situation where a punch was thrown and he threw one back.

At halftime, I said to him, 'Can you fight? Have you got a scrapbook there I can look at? I only want you as a footballer.'

He said, 'No coach. No, it's OK, from now on I'll stick to the rules.'

Out they went, and in the first scrum the other bloke whacked my bloke straight in the mouth. And my bloke stood up and let a couple go. Anyhow, I let him finish the game and afterwards I said to him, 'You didn't do what I suggested you do?'

'Well,' he replied, 'He threw a punch and hit me, but he thought he hit Bunny Reilly, so real quick he said, "Geez Bunny, I didn't know it was you." [I realised then] He wasn't worried about me, but that he wasn't too brave facing someone like Bunny either, so I whacked him back.'

Barry 'Bunny' Reilly was a renowned tough guy, who also went by the nickname 'The Axe'. To me, that incident said a lot about Bunny and players of his kind.

I think Bunny might have trouble surviving today. His specialty was to get 'em in the air, shoulder high. The rules have changed on that and he'd have some problems now.

Ron Coote

I thought a great deal of Ron Coote as a footballer. He was such an effective player, and an outstanding competitor. In earlier days of rugby league the lock forward played a covering role, but I wanted him to make as many tackles as possible, so front-line defence was my philosophy with Ron. He was captain when I first went to Easts, but I lifted that responsibility off him and gave it to John Peard — and the only thing I said to John was, 'You're captain, but you're only captain till you lose it.' After a couple of games I made Arthur Beetson captain, and I said the same thing to him. Arthur asked me, 'How long am I captain for, coach?' And I told him, 'Till you lose it.' As it turned out, Arthur was there for the duration.

Arthur Beetson

The first time I met Arthur Beetson was after I became Easts coach again, for the 1974 season. We had begun pre-season training, and the Kangaroos had been back about a week from their successful tour of England and France. We were training once a week, on a Sunday, and Arthur turned up on this Sunday and trotted around, but the following week he didn't turn up. So I rang him up and said, 'Arthur, if you hadn't turned up for four weeks I would have accepted it because you've had a tough season, but now that you've started to come I expect you there every Sunday.' And he was.

Beetson was a standout, an absolute standout. He was a gamebreaker, something like Wally Lewis. You watch the tape of those State of Origin games from the 1980s; they'd be tough and hard and all of a sudden Lewis would do something, score a try, six points. Beetson did that for Eastern Suburbs. You'd be in there, making tough yards, and then Beetson would put Fairfax away or Brass away or Mullins away. He'd do something that'd open up the whole game and set a trend for the rest of the match. He was an extremely confident footballer, and one of his best assets was that he could read defence. And he could hit. He had a lot of talent, as a player and a captain, and people liked to play with him.

Beetson could handle the responsibility of being captain. Some people are good leaders, but the responsibility affects their game. Others can't handle the responsibility, but still get it because they're a standout player. Beetson didn't fall away in either; in fact, he improved as both a captain and a footballer. He was an ideal captain, because it didn't put any pressure on him, it made him play better. He felt more was expected of him, which was true, but he was concerned with his own game first, which is the principle of a top captain. Much more than the captain, it's the coach's job to look after the team.

• • •

On open letter to Arthur Beetson (1981)

Dear Arthur,

Should you retire from the playing side of football? Should you call it a day? Have your skills and condition started to deteriorate? Is it a case that the mind is willing but the flesh is weak?

There is no doubt that these questions have been constantly in your mind, especially after each game and each tough training session.

Nobody can come up with the answers but yourself.

We have often discussed that the best thing about the game is that there is no place for sympathy. And, like all of us, the decision when to retire draws closer with each passing day.

While this game brings many gratifying moments it also has the complete opposite effect, sometimes almost to the point of drudgery. Many current players, when faced with retirement, will have a much tougher decision to make than yours. Because they must make the full turnaround from competitor to spectator. You, on the other hand, still retain full commitment as director of coaching for your club and as Queensland coach.

When you retire, your team will be deprived of your on-field skills and leadership. You will compensate for this by furthering your off-field ability to coach.

No matter what you decide, everybody, as usual, wishes you well.

Yours sincerely, Jack

•••

In 1984, Eastern Suburbs announced that Arthur Beetson would be their new coach for the following season. In his column in the Daily Mirror, *Jack Gibson published excerpts from an interview he allegedly conducted with Beetson. Here are just a couple of examples of the questions and answers ...*

Jack: Why Eastern Suburbs? You have already been there and done that.

Arthur: Without doubt, they have the best bistro in town, and as Napoleon once said, 'A coach marches on his stomach.'

Jack: Will coaching interfere with your golf?

Arthur: No, the boys will understand that I need diversion and getting in and out of the golf cart is good for physical conditioning.

Jack: Will there be a drop-off in the number of card games that you play?

Arthur: Not necessarily. Exercising the hands and fingers is an important part of therapy when seeking a winning edge ...

Peter Sterling

He was young in years, but he was veteran from the start. Sterling was the type of player who could go to another football team that he'd never heard of, that he'd never seen on video, and he could come in and take the captaincy up and go and play halfback and you'd think he'd been playing five years for them.

Yet he was small and slow. He wasn't quick, Sterling. I see a parallel with Johnny Raper. Raper was small and slow, but what an outstanding player he was. Neither of them would win a footrace for you, but they'd win a football game for you.

It's the simple things that get you home. In this regard, Sterling stood out game after game; maybe he wasn't the most brilliant player, but for consistency he'd win.

Steve Mortimer

Steve Mortimer was probably regarded as a nervous player when he started. But he got better, more solid. I'm sure the success he had along the way helped him. If you were the coach there wouldn't be a game you played against him when you wouldn't be talking about him. He became as good as they get. We were lucky to have him and Sterling around at the same time. They were both excellent, although my view is that Sterling was better. With Sterling there would be games when he would *completely* control the damn thing.

Brett Kenny

Kenny had a lot of things that make a player. He was tough, he was quick, he was an excellent defensive player. He could sniff a try out and was an extremely talented ball handler. A ball that a normal person would drop, Kenny'd catch.

Ron Hilditch

A positive for boys playing a sport like rugby league or rugby union is that they've got to make some decisions they can't hide from. Football can teach them to respond to challenges, physical and mental, in a positive way. Most of the players of my experience have improved, got tougher, as they have gone along. They've become more able to handle some pain and adversity. Some got weaker, but it was many more the other way.

Ron Hilditch was a good example. He wasn't the biggest kid on the block, and he wasn't the heaviest, and he didn't have that special speed or special skills. But there was something about him … as his career went along, everyone came to fear Hilditch a bit. His great quality was his mental strength. He was good at what he did, and he'd always have a positive word to say about people. If you asked him to make a speech it might only be three or four sentences but — always — something good and useful would come out.

On the football field, I remember how we worked on

countering a run-around move that Manly had back in the 1980s, and how when they tried it in the next match, Ronny was there waiting ... and just dropped the bloke with the ball cold. Holy Moly! The bloke was squealing like a pig when he came off the ground. That was Ronny. Give him a job that he liked doing and he'd get it done. There was nothing flash about him, but he made the most of what he had.

Ron Massey

It was important to get people around me who were their own men, who wouldn't say yes because they wanted a job. I didn't want to work with nervous people who didn't have confidence in their own ability to come up with an idea.

So let me say this: I couldn't have got anybody better than Ron Massey to work with as team co-ordinator. He was never a yes man, never under any circumstances would he ever agree with me just to please me. I'd say, 'We're going to use so-and-so on Sunday', and he'd say, 'Well, I wouldn't.' And I'd take notice of what he had to say. Maybe I'd go and watch the video again, because I had to make the final decision, but if he had said, 'I think you should use somebody else,' that had an impact on me.

If you want to know your faults, go and talk to your enemies for a while. They'll tell you. Ron was like my 'enemy'. He filled all the requirements when we needed a co-ordinator. He and I argued many times over the years, but we always came up with a workable solution. He'd pick up things I missed and he helped me through the good times, and the bad times. He contributed — always.

Bob O'Reilly

Everybody liked to play with him. People reckoned he was slow ... but on the football field he could do it all. He was the sort of player you didn't have to give a handful of instructions to, but when he did take instructions into a game he'd stick to them to the letter. At Parramatta during the pre-season of 1981, as we worked through the trials, I said to him one day: 'Robert, I'm going to play you every Sunday — but you've got to turn up every Friday night at 15 stone (95kg).' Or it might have been 15 and a half. You know, he never had a beer after that until the season ended, and he'd turn up every week, never late, and be spot on with his weight. He was a player who set an example.

And as I commented once, he was 'the most exciting two-metre runner in Parramatta's history'.

Neil Hunt

In my years as a coach I was introduced to many footballers. When I first met them, I automatically formed an opinion — sometimes good, sometimes there was little reaction, neither good nor bad.

When I first went to Parramatta I was introduced to a boy called Neil Gilbert Hunt. He had finished the previous year as the first-grade fullback, but after a couple of early trials I decided that he was a nice enough kidlet but did not have what it takes to be a footballer of note.

After a couple of trials I soon had him back in third grade, where I thought he belonged.

At the time, Penrith were interested in his services, and at a much higher salary than he was playing for at the Eels. So I spoke to him one evening at training and said, 'Neil, if you would like to try your luck elsewhere, I'll see to it that you get the opportunity.'

He came back with this replay: 'Well, thanks all the same, but if I'm going to make it I'll make it here at Parramatta.'

Three years later, I watched him be the best winger on the field in a game against Balmain and I thought back. In the seasons since we had that awkward conversation, Neil had played in two first-grade championships, become a leading try-scorer, excellent defender, state representative, outstanding team man. And I'd nearly blown him away.

> **'It's a hard way to make a living, playing against him. He doesn't know the meaning of the word fear ... he doesn't know the meaning of a few other words, too.'**
>
> On Ray Price (1984)

Ray Price

Ray Price played like he trained. Wholeheartedly. All aspects of preparation were important to him.

He wasn't everybody's hero as far as officials were concerned but he has been the model by which other players have been judged.

It may have been talent that has taken him to a level above the rest but clearly it has been persistence and desire to excel that consistently kept him there. *(1984)*

• • •

No one cared what Ray Price did during the week. He might be limping on a Tuesday or a Wednesday night when a decision had to be made: were we going to play him or not? Everyone wanted to know ... is Price playing? Some of the opposition would be looking over their shoulders, hoping that he *might* be wounded. On Sunday, Ray'd be there. There was always a bit of drama around Ray. But he was tough.

Mick Cronin

Mick Cronin will always play on, whatever the game. Roger Kahn, sports reporter and author, once wrote: 'It is fiercely difficult for the sportsman to grow old but to age with dignity and with courage cuts close to what it is to be a man.'

Mick is one of those people.

Even though Michael faced every possible mountain and valley associated with the game, he did it all and won, driving more than a thousand kilometres each week to attend the game and train. He has done this for seven straight years, overcoming major injuries that would have stopped another person.

To me, his real value as a member of a football team did not appear in statistics sheets. It was his ability to lead; not so much by what he did but by his attitude towards others, the game and to himself.

The best team man or men in a club are often indistinguishable to the fan.

To win on a Sunday is the by-product of successful preparation throughout the course of the whole week. This can only be accomplished by players who assume responsibility and take command of themselves.

Parramatta did not lose the championship to Canterbury because Mick missed a couple of goalkicks on Sunday, as some people believe.

They got there in the first place because Michael Cronin continually kicked goals in the art of living and competing.

AFTER THE 1984 GRAND FINAL

•••

Mick Cronin was a little bit quicker than many observers thought he was. However, his greatest asset was that people wanted to play with him and people always played well around him. You could come off and think, 'Gee, the Crow didn't play that good …' But then you'd think, Kenny was on one side of him and he played good, and Ella on the other side, he played good. Those two were beating it out for the game ball. You never saw the blokes playing around Cronin have a poor day. He had that talent, he made people play strong. And he could do the job himself.

'He is about as big as Clive Churchill was when he played and he owns an ugly dog.'

Jack on the 'weaknesses' of Parramatta's Paul Taylor, whom he coached in the 1980s.

George Piggins

I coached George at Souths in the late 1970s, and made him captain. He never had much to say, but he had all the right qualities. He was a dogged, never-say-die player who would just get out there and do what had to be done. And the opposition would know one thing for certain — that George would keep coming at them for the entire game. His influence was all positive. I liked him then and I like him now. We went into business together back then, and we're still in business together today.

Wayne Pearce

In 1983, I was asked who I thought was the best player in the game, apart from those at Parramatta, where I was then coaching. This was how I replied: 'Well, I've got some good players. I would never say we need a new halfback or we need a new lock, but probably the best player playing outside Parramatta is Wayne Pearce. If he wants to come over, I'll give him a trial.'

I always rated 'Junior' Pearce highly. In the '80s, he was just about the best forward going around, a bloke who could really play. He'd get better and better as a game went on. I did actually try to get him to Parramatta at one stage, but loyalty to his home club — the Balmain Tigers — meant a lot to a man like him, and he stayed where he was.

Brad Fittler

In 1990, Fittler was in the team I took down to the second State of Origin game in Melbourne. The five-eighth that I had, Des Hasler, got hurt early in that game and I chose to put the more experienced Andrew Farrar on in his place, leaving Fittler — who was aged 18 then — on the bench. I could have used Fittler, but I didn't. He was entitled to be disappointed with that, but he took it like a man. To me, at the start of his career, that said a lot about him.

I also give Fittler great credit for the way he maintained his composure after he copped a bad cheap shot in the 2002 Grand

Final against the New Zealand Warriors. If he'd have jumped up and reacted badly — as many players would have done — there would have been a real stink ... and maybe a different game. But he didn't. He played on, and played stronger and stronger as the game continued. He handled that situation so well — and I don't think he got the kudos he deserved for doing so. He was a player in control.

Fittler has had a hiccup or two in his career, but he's grown into an outstanding player and an excellent leader. He always has something positive to say. In his latter years at Easts, he's matured into a genuinely great player.

Craig Fitzgibbon

The attitude towards the game of Fitzgibbon, the Sydney Roosters second-rower, is a lesson to any young player. He plays to his potential every week. And there's no rubbish in him at all — he just gets on with the game and the job he has to do. At Cronulla, I worked with his old man, Alan Fitzgibbon, and he was all quality, too.

Today's other stars

I'm often asked who is the best player we have at the moment. Well, Andrew Johns could be the best, but I don't think he's the best magger going around. There's a bit of threat in him. He can certainly play, though.

I rate Darren Lockyer this way: if I was picking a team I'd pick him without hesitation. He's effective in all ways. He can play defence, you don't see him giving penalties away in crucial situations, he doesn't do his block, he respects the people he plays with and he respects the people he plays against. And with the ball in his hands he's got very special talent. There's a lot of Reg Gasnier in this player.

I like Lockyer's Broncos teammate, Gorden Tallis, and I could have used him as captain. But I know I wouldn't have wanted him talking to the referee the way he's talked to Bill Harrigan in the past. I wouldn't have wanted him pointing the finger at somebody in the stand and jumping up and down either. Wayne Bennett knows more about his qualities than I do. He likes him.

Away from Football

Sportspeople like Ian Thorpe should get a medal just for the amount of time they put into the job, let alone for what they achieve. The individual dedication he produces is enormous. And that talent he's got ... I wonder how many people have got that and never use it. He uses his. He's one of those blokes who obviously said to himself, 'Let's find out what I've got.' And he found out all right, and became the best in the world. He gets up at 4.30 every morning to do what he does. He pays his dues. And the expectations on him are enormous. If he hits the water in a race and finishes second or third, people are going to ask, 'What's wrong?' They're going to say that he failed.

Tiger Woods is like Thorpe. He's expected to win every time he steps out there, though maybe because he's a golfer the pressure isn't quite the same as the focus on Thorpe. If Tiger doesn't go quite so well on a given day, we can accept that. Golf is a pressure game. When I play, I get nervous as a cat sometimes. What I've noticed about the bloke with the putter when the pressure is on him is that the ones who can beat it are the ones who don't try to smother it up and pretend they aren't nervous. That's the way. Fear and nerves are part of sport.

From where I sit, it seems that Lleyton Hewitt is getting poorly advised. The way he has spoken to people at times — I'm sure if those situations were reversed he'd go out of his way to make sure it didn't happen again. I'd like to know who he's been listening to ... he couldn't come up with all that stuff himself. Someone's advising him, and I can tell you it's not me. The sad thing is there might be another side to him that's not allowed to come out. He might even be a well-mannered kid. He might have watched too much McEnroe, who in his day was the perfect example of how not to conduct yourself on a tennis court. I believe that if McEnroe *hadn't* gone on like he did, he might have turned out *better* than he did.

Someone else I've been a little disappointed in is the great Australian cricketer Steve Waugh. Just in one area, I must stress. I applaud his wonderful talents, the way he's created an aura about his cricket to the point that you expect him to perform, almost as a matter of course. But the thing I don't like — and I think Steve, as captain, has to accept responsibility for it — is this business of the Australian team having a verbal shot at the opposition. Sledging is a bad habit. I don't see it as being any sort of talent ... I count it as a defect.

In my view, Steve and his men would be better off without it. Sledging wasn't in cricket when I played ... or maybe I wasn't smart enough to think of anything to say. The only sledging that took place back then was one word: 'Howzat!!'

FOURTEEN

One Game Closer to a Win

'There is nothing in the contract that says a football coach has to be sane or a good loser.'

Coaching is extremely personal, more so when you lose. When the team wins, the team did that — that's the way it's got to be, but when things go wrong the coach has got to stand up and take responsibility. These days, a coach is not judged on what type of job he does, but on how many games they win or lose, which is a little sad in many ways because every year they're going to fire the coaches who run last, second last and third last. The only consolation is that with coaches being sacked there's usually an opportunity somewhere else.

•••

When you get beat, you don't want to be shaking hands with anybody. You don't want to be listening to people saying, 'Tough luck, you'll do it next year.' Or: 'Wait until next week, you're just unlucky.' You don't want to listen to that.

I never cared if our dressing room was full when we won, but I certainly preferred it empty when we lost. To me, that's part of the sport scene. That's how it is. A lot of people don't go into dressing rooms when teams get beat because they feel uncomfortable. I don't see that as a snub, I see it as a mark of respect for the team. But I remember one club president in Queensland who once told me that he could never, ever go into the dressing room when his team won but was always there when they lost. And I was thinking, they'd be sick of the sight of *you*.

• • •

There's one thing about a loss, it makes you one game closer to a win.

• • •

Vince Lombardi once said: 'The only time I can reconcile a loss is when every individual on that losing team has played to the best of his ability.'

• • •

In rugby league, there is no adequate substitute for winning.

• • •

It's how you lose. If the game was shot away through lack of discipline or some damn stupid thing I'd do it tough. But if my team had played to its ability, I had something to work with.

• • •

If you haven't played well and accomplished something, but the team has won, you should still feel embarrassed. It's you, personally, who's got to do the job.

In the second Ashes Test of 1984, Australian goalkicker Mal Meninga missed a succession of penalty attempts. Then another chance hit the upright, and Jack was asked what he thought ...

'He's getting closer ...'

I don't know any coach who is going to go to a game and enjoy it. Victory is short lived; even when you win, you're thinking about the next game. As soon as you get out of the dressing room, that's it. You work from match day to match day.

•••

When you win you remember all the good things that happen through the game — when you lose, it's the opposite.

•••

We never worried about what was going to happen down the road. And we didn't spend our next week worrying about why we'd been beaten the Sunday before. What we did was worry about the job at hand, and to take out of that most recent defeat the good things — there can be good things in defeat — and try to make them work for us in the next game.

•••

Positive talking can help. Negative talking has the opposite effect. It will lead you down the path and out the back gate.

You lose.

•••

Remember, losers don't like winners.

PART TWO

FROM THE JACK GIBSON COLLECTION

'I quote others only to better myself …'
MICHEL DE MONTAIGNE,
FRENCH ESSAYIST (1533–92)

ONE

The Coach Says

'Give all the credit away ...'

1. Do what is right. You know the difference, and if you have any doubt, get out the Bible. It's right to be on time, polite, honest, and to remain drug-free.
2. Do your best. We do not help people at all by accepting mediocrity when they are capable of being better. Don't worry about being popular. Many times we don't encourage others to do their best because we are more concerned with our players' appraisal of our efforts than we are with *them*.
3. Treat others as you would like to be treated (the golden rule). I have never seen a team, a family, or a business that can't become better by emphasising love and understanding.

THE THREE SIMPLE RULES FOR SUCCESS OF LOU HOLTZ,
AMERICAN FOOTBALL COACH

I do not believe there is a more worthwhile profession than coaching.

What can be more rewarding than helping young people develop in terms of physical ability, social and emotional maturity, and overall character? And what can be more thrilling than to see your players go on to succeed in their chosen fields?

Few other fields of endeavour provide such an opportunity to affect young people. We must always be mindful of this impact and we must always be ready to accept the responsibilities that go with coaching.

It is our duty to serve as teacher — to provide instruction in the fundamentals of the game and the importance of teamwork. We must also serve as counsellor to assist our players in the process of growing up and to challenge them to become the best they can be on the field and in the classroom.

We must, in short, provide them with the tools and the direction to succeed in life.

VINCENT J. DOOLEY
THE AMERICAN COACHES ASSOCIATION

Love is loyalty. Love is teamwork. Love respects the dignity of the individual. Heart power is the strength of your corporation.

VINCE LOMBARDI, AMERICAN FOOTBALL

Hard work will not guarantee you anything. Without it you don't stand a chance.

PAT RILEY, BASKETBALL

If you must talk, praise your opponent and praise your teammates. Never praise yourself.

JOHN MADDEN, AMERICAN FOOTBALL

Never lie, never cheat, never steal and earn the right to be proud and confident.

JOHN WOODEN, BASKETBALL

Motivation is everything — and the only way to motivate people is to communicate with them. It's important to talk to people in their own language. If you do it well, they'll say, 'He said exactly what I was thinking.' And when they begin to respect you, they'll follow you to the death.

LEE IACOCCA, BUSINESS EXECUTIVE

Winning can be defined as the science of being totally prepared.
GEORGE ALLEN, AMERICAN FOOTBALL

If you don't make a total commitment to whatever you're doing, then you start looking to bail out the first time the boat starts leaking. It's tough enough getting that boat to shore with everybody rowing, let alone when a guy stands up and starts putting his jacket on.

Ability is what you're capable of doing. Motivation determines what you can do. Attitude determines how well you do it.

Self-discipline is an individual's greatest asset.
LOU HOLTZ, AMERICAN FOOTBALL

Whoever wins that flag this year will be the team that trains the hardest, tries the hardest and plays the best.
RON BARASSI, AUSTRALIAN FOOTBALL

JOHN WOODEN'S 'SUCCESS SECRETS'

Fear no opponent. Respect every opponent.

Remember, it's the perfection of the smallest details that makes big things happen.

Keep in mind that hustle makes up for many a mistake.

Be more interested in character than reputation.

Be quick, but don't hurry.

Understand that the harder you work, the more luck you will have.

Know that valid self-analysis is crucial for improvement.

Remember that there is no substitute for hard work and careful planning. Failing to prepare is preparing to fail.

Quoted from Wooden
(McGraw-Hill/Contemporary Books, 1997)

The first time you quit, it's hard. The second time it gets easier. The third time, you don't even have to think about it.
PAUL 'BEAR' BRYANT, AMERICAN FOOTBALL

Nobody who ever gave his best regretted it.
GEORGE HALAS, AMERICAN FOOTBALL

The coach is the team, and the team is the coach. You reflect each other.
SPARKY ANDERSON, BASEBALL

Success isn't permanent, and failure isn't fatal.
MIKE DITKA, AMERICAN FOOTBALL

I think coaching is feeling — it's not x's and o's — it's a feeling. And to me if you're going to be successful in coaching, you have to have a feeling. It's run with your instincts.
KEN HITCHCOCK, ICE HOCKEY

When you build bridges, you can keep crossing them.
RICK PITINO, BASKETBALL

EIGHT RULES FOR SUCCESS ...

Improve every day — as a player, as a person, as a student.

Care about your team mates, friends and family.

Show great effort and enthusiasm.

Associate with only quality people.

Expect more of yourself, always.

Do it right, don't expect less.

Be genuine.

Make discipline a way of life.

Bill Snyder, American Football

If you have players who play through fear you're not going to get any ingenuity out of them.

RED AUERBACH, BASKETBALL

If you don't invest much in the process, then defeat doesn't hurt and winning isn't very exciting.

DICK VERMEIL, AMERICAN FOOTBALL

To me, success isn't outscoring someone; it's the peace of mind that comes from self-satisfaction in knowing you did your best. That's something each individual must determine. You can fool others, but you can't fool yourself.

JOHN WOODEN, BASKETBALL

Many people are surprised to learn that in all my years at UCLA, I never once talked winning. Instead I would tell my players before games, 'When it's over, I want your head up. And there's only one way your head can be up — that's for you to know, not me, that you gave your best effort. If you do that, then the score doesn't really matter, although I have a feeling that if you do give your best, the score will be to your liking.'

JOHN WOODEN, BASKETBALL

I honestly believe that in not stressing winning, as such, we won more than we would have if I'd stressed outscoring opponents.

JOHN WOODEN, BASKETBALL

The four laws of learning are explanation, demonstration, imitation and repetition. The goal is to create a correct habit that can be produced instinctively under great pressure.

To make sure this goal was achieved, I created eight laws of learning, namely: explanation; demonstration; imitation; repetition; repetition; repetition; repetition; repetition; repetition.

JOHN WOODEN, BASKETBALL

TWO

About the Coach

'A wise coach knows everything; a shrewd one, everybody ...'

Tom has the great ability to recognise potential in a player: we have kept players who would not have been around on other contending teams. Tom can see something worth keeping in a mass of humanity. Tactics dwindle in importance to that. What a coach can contribute to a team, in my opinion, is 10 per cent inspiration, 10 per cent motivation, 20 to 30 per cent tactics and 50 to 60 per cent recognition.

> CLINT MURCHISON JR, FORMER DALLAS COWBOYS OWNER, SPEAKING ABOUT HIS COWBOYS COACH, TOM LANDRY

The first thing of importance is to have confidence in yourself, in your abilities.

> KATHARINE GIBBS, EDUCATOR

The coaches who are going to lead things in the future will be the ones who understand their people, and who understand what folks want and that what they need in order to give their best goes way beyond a pay check.

> FRAN TARKENTON, AMERICAN FOOTBALL

> The mediocre coach tells,
> The good coach explains,
> The superior coach demonstrates,
> The great coach inspires.
>
> WILLIAM ARTHUR WARD,
> US AUTHOR AND SCHOLAR

The burdens of coaching are great. One of them is to be unpopular when necessary.

There is something that is much more scarce, something rarer than ability. It is the ability to recognise ability.

ROBERT HALF, BUSINESS CONSULTANT

JUST KIDDING ...

Johnny 'Red' Kerr was an exceptional centre in American college and NBA basketball before becoming the Chicago Bulls first coach in 1966. After the Bulls became the first expansion team to go to the playoffs in their inaugural season, Kerr was named NBA coach of the year. Later, he explained that his biggest test as a coach came during that season, when his biggest-name player was the six foot eight (203cm) Erwin Mueller ...

We had lost seven in a row, and I decided to give a psychological pep talk before a game with the Celtics. I told Bob Boozer to go out and pretend he was the best scorer in basketball. I told Jerry Sloan to pretend he was the best defensive guard. I told Guy Rodgers to pretend he could run an offense better than any other guard. And I told Erwin Mueller to pretend he was the best rebounding, shot-blocking, scoring center in the game.

We lost the game by 17. I was pacing around the locker room afterward trying to figure out what to say when Mueller walked up, put his arm around me, and said, 'Don't worry about it, Coach. Just pretend we won.'

You can't let praise or criticism get to you. It is a weakness to get caught up in either one. Some criticism will be honest and some won't. Some praise you will deserve and some you won't. You have to take both in the same light.

As a coach, the most effective policy is to take the blame for whatever goes wrong. Be smart enough and big enough to look at the situation with complete honesty. What will it get you? Genuine respect.

Coaches who try and impress their players with their 'authority' are displaying leadership by force. Real coaches have no need to advertise their leadership, except by their conduct, sympathy, understanding and ability.

Often, the only difference between the head coach and his assistants is the size of the sandbox.

EVAN B. WELCH

The individual who is mistake-free is also probably sitting around doing nothing. And that's a very big mistake.

A FRESH APPROACH

In 1998, the great Larry Bird was named NBA coach of the year after leading the Indiana Pacers to the playoffs in his first season as an NBA head coach. In an article for The New York Times, *John Wooden paid tribute. Here is part of what Wooden wrote ...*

'Bird's fresh approach to coaching and leadership should be welcome today, when so much has been said about the failure of coaches to assert authority over their players. First, he has shown that emotion is not reliable: getting too high or too low doesn't help win games. And it's a poor way to lead. All too many coaches, at the pro and collegiate levels, rant and rave, often yelling at their players ...

'Bird stays on an even keel. He doesn't lead through fear ...

'As Lincoln said, "There's nothing stronger than gentleness."'

Coaches are divided into two types of people: those who love to talk, and those who hate to listen.

JAMES THORPE

He [John Wooden] would spend a half-hour the first day of practice teaching his men how to put on a sock. 'Wrinkles can lead to blisters,' he'd warn.

These huge players would sneak looks at one another and roll their eyes. Eventually, they'd do it right. 'Good,' he'd say, 'and now for the other foot …'

FROM *WOODEN* (MCGRAW-HILL/CONTEMPORARY BOOKS, 1997)

If you played for him, you played by his rules. Never score without acknowledging a teammate. Treat your opponent with respect. He believed in hopelessly out-of-date stuff that never did anything but win championships. No dribbling behind the back or through the legs. 'There's no need,' he'd say.

EDDIE FUNDERBURK, IN *THE JOHN WOODEN STORY*

No UCLA basketball number was retired under his watch. 'What about the players who wore that number before. Didn't they contribute to the team?' he'd say. No long hair, no facial hair. 'They take too long to dry and you can catch a cold leaving the gym,' he'd say. That one drove his players bonkers. One day, All-American center Bill Walton showed up with a full beard. 'It's my right,' he insisted. Wooden asked if he believed that strongly. Walton said he did. 'That's good, Bill,' coach said. 'I admire people who have strong beliefs and stick to them, I really do. We're going to miss you.' Walton shaved it right then and there.

EDDIE FUNDERBURK, IN *THE JOHN WOODEN STORY*

THREE

Talking and Listening

'There are many times in life when silence is an opinion.'

Give every man thy ear, but few thy voice
WILLIAM SHAKESPEARE, ENGLISH PLAYWRIGHT AND POET

I've never learned anything while I was talking.
LARRY KING, TV INTERVIEWER

Those who hear not the music think the dancers mad.
ANONYMOUS

FORMULA FOR HANDLING PEOPLE

Listen to the others person's story.

Listen to the other person's full story.

Listen to the other person's full story first.

George Marshall, military commander and politician

The coach who listens is not only popular everywhere, but after a while he gets to know something.
WILSON MIZNER, US SCREENWRITER

The more you say, the less people remember.
ANATOLE FRANCE, FRENCH WRITER

Tell people that something is bad and they're not at all sure they want to give it up. Describe it as stupid and they know it's the better part of caution to listen.
DAVID SEABURY, AUTHOR

'Professor, what's the secret to the art of good conversation?' The professor held up an admonishing finger and said, 'Listen.' After a long minute has passed, the sophomore said, 'Well, I'm listening.' And the professor said, 'That's the secret.'

A problem well stated is a problem half-solved.
CHARLES F. KETTERING, US ELECTRICAL ENGINEER AND INVENTOR

A smart coach is one who thinks twice before saying nothing.

It's pretty difficult to keep your mind and your mouth open at the same time.
BITS & PIECES MAGAZINE

On writing: Omit needless words. Vigorous writing is concise. A sentence should contain no unnecessary words, a paragraph no unnecessary sentences, for the same reason that a drawing should have no unnecessary lines and a machine no unnecessary parts.
WILLIAM STRUNK, JR, WRITER

I think the covers are too far apart.
AMBROSE BIERCE, US AUTHOR AND SATIRIST,
WHEN ASKED TO COMMENT ON A PARTICULAR BOOK

My problem is I say what I'm thinking before I think what I'm saying.
>> DR LAURENCE PETER, CANADIAN EDUCATOR

If you don't say anything, you won't be called upon to repeat it.
>> CALVIN COOLIDGE, US PRESIDENT

Nothing is often a good thing to do, and always a clever thing to say.
>> WILLIAM DURANT, US HISTORIAN AND TEACHER

The hardest thing to keep to yourself is an opinion.

We are born with our eyes closed and our mouth open and we spend our whole lives trying to reverse that mistake of nature.
>> DALE TURNER, US RELIGIOUS WRITER

The smartest thing you can do in a negotiation, often, is to keep your mouth shut.
>> ANDREW TOBIAS, US FINANCE JOURNALIST AND BUSINESS CONSULTANT

It is the province of knowledge to speak, and it is the privilege of wisdom to listen.
>> OLIVER WENDELL HOLMES, AMERICAN INTELLECTUAL

Remember, asking questions is the secret of good conversation. I'm curious about everything, and if I'm at a cocktail party, I often ask my favourite question: 'Why?' If a man tells me he and his family are moving to another city: 'Why?' A woman is changing jobs: 'Why?' Someone roots for the Mets: 'Why?'

On my television show, I probably use this word more than any other. It's the greatest question ever asked and it always will be. And it is certainly the surest way of keeping a conversation lively and interesting.
>> LARRY KING, TV INTERVIEWER

Speak only well of people and you will never need to whisper.

The greatest gift you can give another is the purity of your attention.

RICHARD MOSS, US PHYSICIAN

Discussion is an exchange of knowledge; argument an exchange of ignorance.

ROBERT QUILLEN, HUMORIST AND WRITER

We must be silent before we can listen. We must listen before we can learn.

The person who would like to make his dreams come true must stay awake.

RICHARD WHEELER, NOVELIST

Silence is never more golden than when you hold it long enough to get all the facts before you speak.

The way employees treat customers reflects the manner in which they're being treated by management.

JAMES A. PERKINS, EDUCATOR

We must be silent before we can listen.
We must listen before we can learn.
We must learn before we can prepare.
We must prepare before we can serve.
We must serve before we can lead.

William Arthur Ward, US author and scholar

Praise does wonders for the sense of hearing.

Talk is cheap, but you can't buy it back.
LYLE SUSSMAN, MANAGEMENT CONSULTANT, AUTHOR

Sometimes you have to be silent in order to be heard.

All you need in order to get the reputation of being a fascinating person is to say to others, 'How wonderful! Do tell me more.'
DOROTHY DIX, ADVICE COLUMNIST

Among my most prized possessions are the words that I have never spoken.
ORSON REGA CARD

Learn to listen … opportunity sometimes knocks very softly.

If you want to be listened to, you should put time into listening.
MARGE PIERCY, NOVELIST AND POET

Learning begins with listening.
NOAH BEN SHEA, POET AND PHILOSOPHER

FOUR

Leadership

'The distance a person goes is not as important as the direction.'

A leader is a dealer in hope.
NAPOLEON BONAPARTE, FRENCH EMPEROR AND GENERAL

If you just set out to be liked, you would be prepared to compromise on anything at any time, and you would achieve nothing.

MARGARET THATCHER, BRITISH PRIME MINISTER

In my view, quiet confidence gets the best results. Leaders shouldn't do all the talking. Part of their job is to learn, through listening and observing.

JOHN WOODEN, BASKETBALL

The leaders will be those who understand that every member of their team needs to know exactly what is expected of him or her, needs to have access to a score-keeping system that lets one know how one is doing, needs to feel that he or she is contributing to

the team, needs to get constantly and consistently reinforced for that participation and needs to have access to feedback on how the team is going.
FRAN TARKENTON, AMERICAN FOOTBALL

Make big decisions in the calm.
DWIGHT EISENHOWER, US PRESIDENT

Access to power must be confined to men who are not in love with it.
PLATO, GREEK PHILOSOPHER

Leadership is defined by what you do, not who you are.
W.L. GORE, BUSINESS EXECUTIVE

Look at any coach who's made a big change — you can't lead without making sacrifices.
RANDY HOPPER, US ARMY CADET

No person can lead other people except by showing them a future. A coach is a merchant of hope.
NAPOLEON BONAPARTE,
FRENCH EMPEROR AND GENERAL

There is no necessary connection between the desire to lead and the ability to lead, and even less the ability to lead somewhere that will be to the advantage of the led.
BERGEN EVANS, EDUCATOR

I praise loudly. I blame softly.
CATHERINE 'THE GREAT', RUSSIAN EMPRESS

There are two ways you can get others to do what you want: compulsion or persuasion. Compulsion is the method of slavery. Persuasion is the method of free people.

HOW TO RECOGNISE LEADERSHIP

Leaders don't force other people to go along with them; they bring them along.

Leaders get commitment from others by giving it themselves, by building an environment that encourages creativity, and by operating with honesty and fairness.

Leaders demand much of others, but they also give much of themselves. They are ambitious — not only for themselves, but also for those they work with. They seek to attract, retain and develop other people to their full abilities.

Good leaders aren't 'lone rangers'. They realise that success requires the combined talents and efforts of many people. Leadership is the catalyst for transforming those talents into results.

Successful leaders are emotionally and intellectually oriented to the future — not wedded to the past. They have a hunger to take responsibility, to innovate and initiate. They want to move forward to create something new.

Leaders provide answers as well as direction, offer strength as well as dedication, and speak from experience as well as understanding the problems they face and the people with whom they work.

Leaders are flexible rather than dogmatic. They believe in unity rather than conformity, and they strive to achieve consensus out of conflict.

From a United Technologies Corporation advertisement

You can employ men and hire staff to work for you, but you will have to win their hearts to have them work with you.

WILLIAM J.H. BOETCKER,
CLERGYMAN

Keep away from people who try to belittle your ambition. Small people always do that, but the really great make you feel that you, too, can become great.

MARK TWAIN, US WRITER

Even a two-car parade gets fouled up, if you don't decide ahead of time who's going to lead.

ZIG ZIGLAR, MOTIVATOR

To persuade requires an understanding of how people tick, of what motivates them — a knowledge of human nature.

What a man dislikes in his superiors, let him not display in the treatment of his inferiors.

TSANG SIN,
CHINESE SCHOLAR AND PHILOSOPHER

Seventy psychologists were once asked: 'What is the most essential thing for a supervisor to know about human nature?' Two-thirds said that motivation — an understanding of what makes people think, feel and act as they do — was uppermost.

If you understand what motivates people you have at your command the most powerful tool for dealing with them.

Once you have someone's trust ... they don't want to disappoint you. Then leading becomes easy.

Leaders don't force people to follow — they invite them on a journey.

CHARLES S. LAUER,
BUSINESSMAN AND PUBLISHER

A true coach has the confidence to stand alone, the courage to make tough decisions, and the compassion to listen to the needs of others. He does not set out to be a leader, but becomes one by the quality of his actions and the integrity of his intent. In the end, leaders are much like eagles — they don't flock, you find them one at a time.

> The true leader is always led.
> CARL JUNG, SWISS PSYCHIATRIST

A plausible technique of breaking up a batting slump: My guess is that a player is told what he is doing wrong or shown moves or videotapes of himself as he strikes out or grounds out easily. I suggest instead, he be shown a short film of himself hitting home runs.
ON HOW TO HIT HOME RUNS IN LIFE

True coaches are those who lead by example rather than by intimidation. The whole point of leadership is having power with people — not lording it over them.
DONNA KARLIN, PERSONAL DEVELOPMENT COACH

The real leader has no need to lead — he is content to point the way.
HENRY MILLER, WRITER

If you're riding ahead of the herd, take a look back every now and then to make sure it's still there.
WILL ROGERS, US ACTOR

Here is the very heart and soul of the matter: If you look to lead, invest at least 40 per cent of your time managing yourself, your ethics, character, principles, purpose, motivation and conduct. Invest at least 30 per cent managing those with authority over you, and 15 per cent managing your peers. Use the remainder to induce those you 'work for' to understand and practise the theory. I use the terms 'work for' advisedly, for if you don't understand that you should be working for your mislabelled 'subordinates', you haven't understood anything. Lead yourself, lead your superiors. Lead your peers and free your people to do the same. All else is trivia.

FROM *FAST COMPANY* MAGAZINE

Leadership is not a spectator sport. Leaders don't sit in the stands and watch. Neither are they in the game substituting for the players. Leaders coach. They show others how to behave, both on and off the field. They demonstrate what is important by how they spend their time, by the priorities on their agenda, by the questions they ask, by the people they see, the places they go, and the behaviour and results that they recognise and reward.

Every step a leader takes and every move he or she makes is watched. Leadership is a dramatic art. Leaders are always on stage. Leaving by example is visible management. Employees can see what is expected and required of them by observing what their boss does.

JAMES KOUZES, AUTHOR AND MOTIVATIONAL SPEAKER

The great leaders in basketball have never been afraid of change, and they have led from the strength of their own convictions. And, above all, they have brought out the best in the people they led.

BILL BRADLEY, US BASKETBALLER AND POLITICIAN

In the place where there is a leader, do not seek to become a leader. In the place where there is no leader, strive to become a leader.

FROM THE TALMUD, JEWISH WRITINGS

A leader is more fearless, more courageous than anyone else around. A leader sees the vision, communicates its possibilities, believes in its achievements, inspires others to contribute their best, motivates others to contribute their best, motivates others to want to belong, stretches and pushes people, and demonstrates the confidence of victorious achievement of the vision …

LEE BARR & NORMA BARR, IN THEIR BOOK,
THE LEADERSHIP EQUATION (EAKIN PUBLICATIONS, 1989)

> ## A LACK OF LEADERSHIP?
>
> *The three things you can do to make sure that you are not demoralised by lack of leadership ...*
>
> First, set clear-cut standards of conduct and responsibility. People should know exactly what is expected of them, and all should be judged against the same set of values.
>
> Second, don't spare the bad apples in your group. Have the guts to correct the situation before it contaminates your entire organisation.
>
> Third, reward the good. Rewards to those who deserve them serve to maintain their morale and enthusiasm. They also let those who are loafing know where they stand too.

Good coaches inspire others with confidence in their leadership; great coaches inspire others with confidence in themselves. 'You won't be dropped if you make a wrong decision,' the coach of a football club tells his players. 'You'll only be dropped if you make no decision.'

> Example has more followers than reason.
> CHRISTIAN BOVEE, US AUTHOR

A leader takes people where they want to go. A great leader takes people where they don't necessarily want to go but ought to be.
ROSALYNN CARTER, WIFE OF THE 39TH US PRESIDENT

One of the keys to playing the game is to understand that it's not as important to know where the puck is at any given time as to know where it will be.

WAYNE GRETZKY, ICE HOCKEY

FIVE

Building a Team

'The firefighter holding the ladder is as important as
the firefighter holding the hose.'

There are plenty of teams in every sport that have great players and never win titles. Most of the time, those players aren't willing to sacrifice for the greater good of the team. The funny thing is, in the end their unwillingness to sacrifice only makes individual goals more difficult to achieve ... Talent wins games, but teamwork and intelligence win championships.

MICHAEL JORDAN, BASKETBALL

(To paraphrase the legendary actor Jimmy Stewart ...) I never think of my team as players. I think of them as partners.

Everybody wants to be a championship team, but nobody wants to come to practice.

BOBBY KNIGHT, BASKETBALL

Every coach wants to have a staff that works together as a team. But in many organisations there are one or two people who are mavericks. They're on the opposite side of every majority consensus, always ready to point out flaws in proposed plans, always suggesting things that no one else considers appropriate.

People like this can be uncomfortable to have around. Egotism or just plain contrariness may motivate them. But it's also quite possible that they are sometimes right.

> My best friend is the one who brings out the best in me.
> HENRY FORD, FOUNDER, FORD MOTOR COMPANY

The most important measure of how good a game I played was how much better I'd made my teammates play.
> BILL RUSSELL, BASKETBALL

Too much harmony and agreement in an organisation can invite trouble. People with different views may force you to take another look at a plan and consider angles you might not have considered.

Many ideas grow better when transplanted into another mind than the one where they sprang up.
> OLIVER WENDELL HOLMES, AMERICAN INTELLECTUAL

Players are usually willing to pull harder when it's in support of a mission or vision they care about. Team spirit wins games — team members need time to develop trust in the organisation. The most important signal management can send is to empower the players to make decisions. Let those on the field play the game. Don't let rules and policies outweigh suggestions.

> Players have one thing in common: they are all different.
> ROBERT ZEND, WRITER

When building a team, I always search first for people who love to win. If I can't find any of those, I look for people who hate to lose.
H. ROSS PEROT, BUSINESS EXECUTIVE

> You can't tell how much spirit a team has until it starts losing.
> ROCKY COLAVITO, BASEBALL

A bad attitude is the worst thing that can happen to a group of people. It's infectious.

ROGER ALLAN RABY

For the best results, coaches must have some confidence in the ability of people to do their jobs. Maybe not as well or exactly the way they would do it themselves, but well enough to satisfy the demands of the job. Frequently, if they have an open mind, they will find that their associates will do the job even better than they could have done it.

FAMILY TIES

At one point during a game, the coach said to one of his young players, 'Do you understand what co-operation is? What a team is?'

The little boy nodded in the affirmative. 'Do you understand that what matters is whether we win together as a team?'

The little boy nodded yes. 'So,' the coach continued, 'when a strike is called, or you're out at first, you don't argue or curse or attack the umpire. Do you understand all that?'

Again the little boy nodded. 'Good,' said the coach. 'Now go over there and explain it to your mother.'

The Executive Speaker *newsletter*

If you don't trust your associates to know what's going on, they'll know you don't really consider them partners.

SAM WALTON, FOUNDER WAL-MART DISCOUNT STORES

> In order that people may be happy
> in their work or sport,
> these three things are needed —
> they must be fit for it;
> they must not do too much of it; and
> they must have a sense of success in it.
>
> JOHN RUSKIN, BRITISH ART AND SOCIAL COMMENTATOR

The most important single ingredient in the formula of success is knowing how to get along with people.

THEODORE ROOSEVELT, US PRESIDENT

Teamwork starts with sharing information. Teamwork is a product of sharing — sharing interests, responsibilities and credit. It's something that no strictly self-centred coach can hope to achieve. Coaches who are concerned primarily with advancing their own image and importance might as well forget about teamwork. They are not going to inspire any.

People come into your life for a reason, a season, or a lifetime; when you figure out which it is, you'll know exactly what to do.

MICHELLE VENTOR

With a winning team, you just have to show them where the next mountain is.

BILL PARCELLS, AMERICAN FOOTBALL

In the game of life, I'm not even interested in the best seats on the 50-yard line. I want to be a team player. I came to play the game.

FRANK CANDY, MOTIVATIONAL SPEAKER

The best morale exists when you rarely hear the word mentioned. When you hear a lot of talk about it, it's usually very poor.
DWIGHT EISENHOWER, US PRESIDENT

Mickey Mantle once told Yankee teammate Tony Kubeck he wanted one thing written on his tombstone: 'I was a good teammate.'
KEN MCMILLAN

The way to get things done is not to mind who gets the credit for doing them.
BENJAMIN JOWETT, ENGLISH SCHOLAR

Whatever your past has been, you have a spotless future.
MELANIE GUSTAFSON, US HISTORIAN

SIX

Great Expectations

'The best way to predict the future is to create it.'

For a long time it had seemed to me that life was about to begin — real life! But there was always some obstacle in the way, something to be gotten through first, some unfinished business — time to be served, a debt to be paid. Then life would begin. At last it dawned on me that obstacles were my life.

FATHER ALFRED D'SOUZA

> Losers visualise the penalties of failure.
> Winners visualise the rewards of success.
> ROB GILBERT, EDITOR, *BITS & PIECES*

IMPOSSIBLE! That is one word that blocks all human progress

DR DENNIS P. KIMBRO, AUTHOR AND EDUCATOR

Outstanding coaches go out of the way to boost the self-esteem of their personnel. If people believe in themselves, it's amazing what they can accomplish.

SAM WALTON, FOUNDER WAL-MART DISCOUNT STORES

Players who learn they've been kept in the dark lose confidence in coaches quickly.
>   MARGARET WHEATLEY, AUTHOR, MANAGEMENT CONSULTANT

Failure waits for those who stay with some success made yesterday. Tomorrow you must try once more and even harder than before.

You can buy people's time; you can buy their physical presence at a given place; you can even buy a measured number of their skilled muscular motions per hour. But you cannot buy enthusiasm — you cannot buy loyalty — you cannot buy the devotion of hearts, mind, or souls — you must earn these.
>   CLARENCE FRANCIS

Nothing is more dangerous than an idea when it is the only one you have.
>   EMILE CHARTIER

A player's performance tends to rise or fall to meet the coach's expectations.
>   FRANK F. HUPPE, BUSINESS CONSULTANT AND MOTIVATOR

Deliver more than you promise, rather than promise more than you can deliver.

Many coaches spoil the work just as it nears completion. They get eager. They get invested in certain outcomes. They become anxious and make mistakes. This is a time for care and consciousness. Don't do too much. Don't be too helpful. Don't worry about getting credit for having done something.

Two ways to be rich:
Have all you want. Be satisfied with what you have.

Leadership magazine

> What do people value most in a coach?
>
> **Most of us want someone who is honest, truthful and straightforward, someone we know really has our interest at heart, someone we can trust.**
>
> *Leadership* magazine

Half of getting what you want is knowing what you must give up to get it.
ROBERT ANTHONY, PSYCHOLOGIST AND MOTIVATOR

Before following the coach, find out who the coach is.
DAVE WEINBAUM, PHILOSOPHER

Players are generally most productive and efficient when they have a clear idea what is expected of them.

We must play the hand we're dealt. And not the one we wish we had.
ART BUCK

If a man could have half of his wishes, he would double his trouble.
BENJAMIN FRANKLIN, SCIENTIST AND DIPLOMAT

Because the wise coach has no expectations, no outcome can be called a failure. Paying attention, allowing a natural unfolding and standing back most of the time, the leader sees the event arrive at a satisfactory conclusion.

The first time I walked into a trophy shop I looked around and thought to myself, 'This guy is good.'
FRED WOLF

The coach's mind must remain open at all times. If you do not expect the unexpected, you will not find it.

HERACLIUS, BYZANTINE EMPEROR

The study of followership is an important avenue to understanding leadership. If a person will analyse his experiences and attitudes as a follower, he will obtain a new concept of coaching.

DR EMORY BOGARDUS, US SOCIOLOGIST

A certain amount of permanent dissatisfaction with one's talent is probably a healthy thing. The coach who is totally satisfied with his work will never reach his potential.

There are two ways to slide easily through life: to believe everything or to doubt everything. Both ways save us from thinking.

ALFRED KORZYBSKI, AMERICAN SEMANTICIST

Nothing happens until someone steps forward and says, 'You can count on me.'

ROB GILBERT, EDITOR, *BITS & PIECES*

My interest is in the future because I am going to spend the rest of my life there.

CHARLES F. KETTERING, US ELECTRICAL ENGINEER AND INVENTOR

As coach you'll never have all the information you need to make a decision. If you did, it would be a foregone conclusion, not a decision.

DAVID MAHONEY JR, PHILOSOPHER

Blessed are those who give without remembering and take without forgetting.

ELIZABETH BIBESCO, WRITER

SEVEN

The Best Advice

'Don't expect others to listen to your advice and ignore your example.'

Know when to tune out. If you listen to too much advice, you may wind up making other people's mistakes.

ANN LANDERS, AMERICAN ADVICE COLUMNIST

As a general rule, people ask for advice on coaching only in order not to follow it; or if they do follow it, in order to have someone to blame for giving it.

Advice is what we ask for when we already know the answer, but wish we didn't.

ERICA JONG, NOVELIST

Nobody can give you wiser advice than yourself.

MARCUS TULLIUS CICERO, ROMAN STATESMAN

The trouble with giving advice is that people want to repay you.

VERN MCLELLAN, HUMORIST AND AUTHOR

> Show up on time.
> Do what you say you will do.
> Finish what you start.
> Say please and thank you.
> CANADIAN BUSINESS CONSULTANT DAN SULLIVAN'S
> FOUR RULES FOR BUSINESS SUCCESS

No one wants advice — especially the coach — we only want corroboration.

JOHN STEINBECK, AUTHOR

> Many coaches receive advice.
> Only the wise profit from it.
> PUBLILIUS SYRUS, ROMAN WRITER, PHILOSOPHER

When you're the coach, it's queer how ready people always are with advice in any real or imaginary emergency, and no matter how many times experience has shown them to be wrong, they continue to set forth their opinions, as if they had received them from the Almighty.

ANNIE SULLIVAN, TEACHER

Over the years I've learned a lot about coaching staffs and one piece of advice I would pass on to a young coach — or a corporation executive or even a bank president — is this: don't make them in your image. Don't even try. My assistants don't look alike, think alike, or have the same personalities. And I sure don't want them all thinking the way I do. You don't strive for sameness, you strive for balance.

PAUL 'BEAR' BRYANT, AMERICAN FOOTBALL

> Don't let anyone outwork you.
> DEREK JETER, SHORTSTOP FOR THE NEW YORK YANKEES, WHEN ASKED WHAT
> WAS THE BEST ADVICE HIS FATHER HAD GIVEN HIM

> Nothing is so simple that it can't be misunderstood.
> *JUNIOR LEAGUE* MAGAZINE

Let it never be said of you, 'I thought he would never finish.' Follow the advice I was given when singing in supper clubs: 'Get off while you're ahead; always leave them wanting more.' Make sure you have finished speaking before your audience has finished listening.

DOROTHY SARNOFF, SPEECH EXPERT AND AUTHOR

Advice is like snow: the softer it falls, the longer it dwells upon, and the deeper it sinks into the mind.

SAMUEL T. COLERIDGE, ENGLISH POET

Take it from me, do not advise too much. Do the job yourself. That is the only advice you can give to others. Do it and others will follow.

JAWAHARLAL NEHRU, INDIAN PRIME MINISTER

Don't tell a man how to do a thing. Tell him what you want done and he'll surprise you with his ingenuity.

GENERAL GEORGE PATTON

My best advice came from a friend immediately after I was named to a top country coaching job. 'Son, in this job you will have thousands of opportunities to keep your mouth shut. Take advantage of all of them.'

DEWEY KNIGHT

EIGHT

Seats of Learning

'It's easier to be wise for others than for ourselves.'

Champions once sat where you are sitting, kid. The Football Hall of Fame (and every other Hall of Fame) is filled with names of people who sat, week after week, without getting a spot of mud on their well-laundered uniforms. Generals, senators, surgeons, prize-winning novelists, professors, business executives, started on the bench too.

Keep your eye on the game. Watch for defensive lapses. Look for offensive opportunities. If you don't think you're in a great spot wait and see how many kids would like to take it away from you at next spring practice.

What you do from the bench this season could put you on the field next season as a player, or back in the grandstand as a spectator.

DICK KERR, WRITING ABOUT THE 'KID SITTING ON THE END OF THE BENCH' AS PART OF A SERIES OF MOTIVATIONAL ADVERTISEMENTS FOR UNITED TECHNOLOGIES CORPORATION

Many people believe that stories are told to put people to sleep. I tell mine to wake them up.

RABBI NACHMAN OF BRESLOV, TEACHER, WRITER

FINDING THE RIGHT PEOPLE

Learning to pick the right people for the right job is one of the most important things any coach does. In fact success depends upon it.

Some coaches seem to have a knack for picking the right people.

The first step, obviously, is a careful analysis of the job itself. What abilities are required? What kind of personality or temperament? How essential is previous experience? What kind of person can you imagine doing this job well?

Next, what candidates do you have available? How do their abilities and personalities fit the requirements? If you're unsure of their abilities, is there any way you can test to find out? Could any of them meet the requirements if given some special training?

Sometimes it's obvious that none of the available candidates could fill the bill. That's where foresight comes into the picture. It should have been used a long time ago to foresee and avoid such a predicament. No one can put the right person in the right job unless the right person is available.

I never thought about losing but now that it's happened, the only thing to do is do it right. We all have to take defeats in life.

MUHAMMAD ALI,
WORLD HEAVYWEIGHT BOXING CHAMPION

Never mistake knowledge for wisdom. One helps you make a living and the other helps you make a life.

SANDRA CAREY

As coaches we have a responsibility to grow close to our learners and to help them know themselves.

KAYE THORNE, AUTHOR AND TRAINER

Nothing fails like success because we don't learn from it. We learn only from failure.
> KENNETH EWART BOULDING, ECONOMIST, AUTHOR, PEACE ACTIVIST

When you say yes, say it quickly. But always take a half-hour to say no, so you can understand the other fellow's side.
> CARDINAL FRANCIS SPELLMAN, ARCHBISHOP OF NEW YORK

It's the little things that make the big things possible. Only close attention to the fine details of any operation makes the operation first-class.
> J. WILLARD MARRIOTT, BUSINESS EXECUTIVE

You teach best what you most need to learn.
> RICHARD BACH, AUTHOR

We often consider that joy is essential. I don't know of any other culture so bent on pleasure. We are lost in the pursuit of pleasure so much that we forget there are other things. Joy is a great teacher, but so is despair. Hope is a great teacher, but so is disillusionment — to deny yourself any of these is not experiencing life totally.
> LEO BUSCAGLIA, AMERICAN PSYCHOLOGIST AND WRITER

I have learned silence from the talkative, toleration from the intolerant, and kindness from the unkind. Yet, strange, I am ungrateful to these teachers.
> KAHLIL GIBRAN, ARAB-AMERICAN MYSTIC, PAINTER AND POET

Perhaps the most valuable result of all education is the ability to make yourself do the thing you have to do when it ought to be done, whether you like it or not. It is the first lesson that ought to be learned and is probably the last lesson a person learns thoroughly.
> THOMAS HUXLEY, ENGLISH BIOLOGIST

Great minds discuss ideas, average minds discuss events, small minds discuss people.

REAR ADMIRAL HYMAN RICKOVER

The thoughts that come often unsought, and as it were, drop into the mind, are commonly the most valuable of any we have.

JOHN LOCKE, BRITISH PHILOSOPHER

Nanin, a Japanese master during the Meija era, received a university professor who came to inquire about Zen. Nanin served tea. He poured his visitor's cup full, and then kept on pouring. The professor watched the overflow until he no longer could restrain himself. 'It is overfull. No more will go in!'

'Like this cup,' Nanin said, 'you are full of your own opinions and speculations. How can I show you Zen unless you first empty your cup?'

MARC DE SMEDT, AUTHOR

First forget inspiration — habit is more appendable. Habit will sustain you whether you're inspired or not. Habit is persistence in practice.

OCTAVIA BUTLER, SCIENCE FICTION WRITER

The real danger is not that computers will begin to think like men, but that men will begin to think like computers.

SYDNEY J. HARRIS, SYNDICATED COLUMNIST

After I won the Olympics my Mom used to tell me, 'Always believe in yourself — but never, ever believe your own PR.'

PEGGY FLEMING, ICE SKATING

Wonder, rather than doubt, is the root of knowledge.

ABRAHAM HESCHEL, AUTHOR AND TEACHER

Rules are for when thinking stops.

H.D. MALLORY

THE GETTING OF WISDOM

Patience is the companion of wisdom.
St Augustine, Roman priest

It is the province of knowledge to speak and it is the privilege of wisdom to listen.
Oliver Wendell Holmes, American intellectual

You can tell whether a coach is clever by his answers. You can tell whether a coach is wise by his questions.
Naguib Mahfouz, Egyptian writer

No sport can progress and grow without leadership. In the final analysis, coaching is the only real advantage one organisation has over another in a competitive society.

Wise coaches profit more from fools than fools from wise men; for the wise men shun the mistakes of fools, but fools do not imitate the successes of the wise.
Cato the Elder, Roman general and statesman

The stupid neither forgive nor forget; the naïve forgive and forget; the wise forgive but do not forget.
Dr Thomas Szasz, professor of psychiatry

The hardest thing to learn in life is which bridge to cross and which to burn.

DAVID RUSSELL

We learn from experience that we never learn from experience.

GEORGE BERNARD SHAW, IRISH PLAYWRIGHT

> Be wiser than other people if you can, but do not tell them so.
> *Lord Chesterfield, British statesman (in a letter to his son)*
>
> The art of being wise is the art of knowing what to overlook.
> *William James, US psychologist and philosopher*
>
> Wise coaches learn when they can. Fools learn when they must.
> *Duke of Wellington, British Prime Minister and general*
>
> Circumstances are the rulers of the weak; they are but the instruments of the wise.
> *Samuel Lover, Irish painter and novelist*
>
> A wise coach does at once what a fool does at last.
> *Baltasar Gracián, Spanish philosopher and writer*
>
> 1. Enthusiasm is not a random mood; it's a daily choice.
> 2. Taking time to listen to others is a rare and special talent.
> 3. Self-belief is a simple matter of focusing on what you do have.
> 4. A sincere compliment is the least expensive and most valuable gift a coach can offer.
> 5. Wisdom is always realising that the only time you can ever love is now.
>
> *Joe Takash, motivational speaker*

You can learn little from victory. You can learn everything from defeat.

CHRISTY MATHEWSON, BASEBALL

Experience is a good teacher, but her fees are very high.

DEAN WILLIAM RALPH INGE, ENGLISH PRELATE

When I was a kid I drew like Michelangelo. It took me years to learn to draw like a kid.
PABLO PICASSO, PAINTER AND SCULPTOR

If you can keep your head when all about you are losing theirs, it's just possible that you haven't grasped the situation.
JEAN KERR, AUTHOR AND DRAMATIST

The things that hurt instruct.
BENJAMIN FRANKLIN, SCIENTIST AND DIPLOMAT

No idea is so antiquated that it was not once modern. No idea is so modern that it will not someday be antiquated.
ELLEN GLASGOW, NOVELIST

Statistics are no substitute for judgment.
HENRY CLAY, US POLITICIAN

If you want to build a ship, don't drum up people together to collect wood and don't assign them tasks and work, but rather teach them to long for the endless immensity of the sea.
ANTOINE DE SAINT-EXUPÉRY, FRENCH AVIATOR AND WRITER

One of the most important things I ever learned came late in life. It was how to say I don't know.
W. SOMERSET MAUGHAM, ENGLISH NOVELIST AND DRAMATIST

Everything that irritates us about others can lead us to an understanding of ourselves.
CARL JUNG, SWISS PSYCHIATRIST

Experience tells you what to do; confidence allows you to do it.
STAN SMITH, TENNIS

The biggest idiot can sometimes ask the questions the smartest person can't answer. In politics, stupidity is not a handicap.
NAPOLEON BONAPARTE, FRENCH EMPEROR AND GENERAL

The most important skill to acquire now is learning how to learn.
JOHN NAISBITT, US BUSINESS WRITER AND SOCIAL RESEARCHER

Asking the right questions takes as much skill as giving the right answers.
ROBERT HALF, BUSINESS CONSULTANT

Do not put faith in what statistics say until you have carefully considered what they do not say.
WILLIAM W. WATT

Strange but true — 40 per cent of all statistics are meaningless!

NINE

Facing Facts

'A mistake not corrected is just another mistake.'

You are never really playing against an opponent — you are playing against yourself.

ARTHUR ASHE, TENNIS

> Don't build me a watch, just tell me the time.
> CHARLIE MCCARTHY

Good coaches aren't reluctant to talk to their people about their future prospects. But they're realistic when they do — they don't create false hopes by painting too rosy a view.

You, the coach, will do foolish things, but do them with enthusiasm.

COLETTE, FRENCH NOVELIST

Of what help is anyone who can only be approached with the right words?

ELIZABETH BIBESCO, WRITER

Stand up so you will be seen. Speak up so you will be heard. And then sit down so you'll be appreciated.

JOHN DAVIES

What we see depends mainly on what we look for.
JOHN LUBBOCK, ENGLISH POLITICIAN, SCIENCE WRITER

I've spoken my mind even when I knew that what I said might be unpopular, because I believe that to speak your mind is essential to take part in a controversy is important. It has never been my nature to sit back and keep quiet for fear of treading on somebody's toes.

If, for a good cause, you must make an enemy, accept that fact. As long as your conscience is clear, you will find that you have strengthened not only your determination but your character.

LILLI PALMER

Self-delusion is pulling in your stomach when you step on the scales.

PAUL SWEENEY

Eventually everyone has to face the facts. That's why one of the basic policies of a good coach is not to mislead people. Any benefit to be gained from creating false hopes will be lost several times over when these expectations don't come true.

I believe in so many things that it would take a book to tell about them. Especially so I believe that the greatest pleasure and privilege which a grown person can achieve is to be allowed to enter into the beautiful garden which is the mind of a child.

J. LINTON RIGG, SAILOR AND DESIGNER OF YACHTS

When we doubt, tell the truth.
MARK TWAIN, US WRITER

Men stumble over the truth from time to time, but most pick themselves up and hurry off as if nothing happened.

WINSTON CHURCHILL, BRITISH PRIME MINISTER

If you have 'class', you don't need much of anything else. If you don't have it, no matter what else you have — it doesn't make much difference.

HOWARD E. FERGUSON, MOTIVATIONAL AUTHOR

To see a man beaten not by a better opponent but by himself, is a tragedy.

CUS D'AMATO, BOXING TRAINER

There are two kinds of players who never amount to very much; those who cannot do what they are told, and those who can do nothing else.

CYRUS H.K. CURTIS, US PUBLISHER

It is very foolish to insist on being the only one who is right.

FRANCOIS DE LA ROCHEFOUCAULD, FRENCH CLASSICAL WRITER

The closest to perfection a person ever comes is when he fills out a job application form.

STANLEY J. RANDALL

Experience is the name every coach gives to his mistakes

OSCAR WILDE, IRISH WRITER

From the coach ...

Honesty's the best policy;
I can only please one person per day;
Today is not your day;
Tomorrow is not looking good either.

More coaches have been made great by crosses than by crowns. Conversely, more people have been made soft, even ruined, by crowns than by crosses.
RICHARD CARDINAL CUSHING, ARCHBISHOP OF BOSTON

What is the one thing that destroys most coaches? That something is a continually growing belief in their individual infallibility — the thought that only they can see the light that is hidden from everyone else. 'Why am I the only one who knows how to do anything?' these coaches keep asking.
PHILIP B. CROSBY, MANAGEMENT CONSULTANT

The less a coach knows, the more sure they are that they know everything.
JOYCE CARY, IRISH WRITER

We have to accept that the coach's journey demands refusal and failure before it can be completed.
MARGARET WHEATLEY, AUTHOR, MANAGEMENT CONSULTANT

The two hardest things to handle in coaching are failure and success.

Lost time is never found again.
THELONIOUS MONK, US PIANIST AND COMPOSER

A coach of character knows what his limitations are — but he doesn't accept them.

From the errors of others a wise coach corrects his own.
PUBLILIUS SYRUS, ROMAN WRITER, PHILOSOPHER

The greatest mistake a coach can make in life is to be continually fearing he will make one.
ELBERT GREEN HUBBARD, US BUSINESSMAN AND WRITER

All coaches must face crisis where their own strength of character is the enemy.
> RICHARD REEVES,
> US JOURNALIST AND ESSAYIST

If you think education is expensive, coach, try ignorance.
> DEREK BOK, PRESIDENT, HARVARD UNIVERSITY

Speak when you're angry, and you'll make the best speech you'll ever regret.
> HENRY WARD BEECHER, AMERICAN CLERGYMAN

One of the tests of a coach is the ability to recognise a problem before it becomes an emergency.

In every organisation, whether it is a family of four or a company of 100,000, the only way to keep a high level of enthusiasm is to build adequate corridors for grievances.
> ALAN LOY MCGINNIS,
> CORPORATE CONSULTANT

Words that will guarantee failure: COULD ... SHOULD ... WON'T.
> JIM ROHN, MOTIVATIONAL SPEAKER

In coaching, the common error is to try to correct too many faults at the same time — just work at one thing at a time.

The greatest of faults, I should say, is to be conscious of none.
> THOMAS CARLYLE, SCOTTISH AUTHOR AND HISTORIAN

When mistakes occur — no matter how serious — don't immediately set out with the idea of blaming somebody. That's unimportant.

The tragedy is that so many people look for self-confidence and self-respect everywhere except within themselves and so they fail in their search.

NATHANIEL BRANDEN, PROFESSIONAL THERAPIST AND AUTHOR

It is the job of a coach to make it easy to do the right thing, difficult to do the wrong thing.

Do not condemn the judgment of another because it differs from your own. May you not both be in error?

DANDEMIS, INDIAN PHILOSOPHER

Any fool can criticise, condemn and complain, and most fools do.

DALE CARNEGIE, US WRITER

A new idea is delicate. It can be dulled by a sneer or a yawn; it can be stabbed to death by a quip and worried to death by a frown on the right man's brow.

CHARLES BROWER

An expert is a person who has made all the mistakes which can be made in a very narrow field.

NIELS BOHR, DANISH PHYSICIST

Don't accept your dog's admiration as conclusive evidence that you are wonderful.

ANN LANDERS, AMERICAN ADVICE COLUMNIST

Mistakes are a fact of life. It is the response to the error that counts.

NIKKI GIOVANNI, US AUTHOR AND POET

TEN

Persist!

'If you weather the storm, you'll reach the port.'

> The important thing is not to stop questioning.
> ALBERT EINSTEIN, PHYSICIST

Fame is a vapour, popularity an accident, riches take wings. Only one thing endures and that is character.

> ABRAHAM LINCOLN, US PRESIDENT

Persistence is not inherited. It's a state of mind — an attitude. And since it is an attitude, it's something each of us can develop.

Life ain't in holding a good hand, but in playing a poor hand well.

> JACK KING, GAMBLER

Do not spoil what you have by desiring what you have not; but remember that what you now have was once among the things you only hoped for.

> EPICURUS, GREEK PHILOSOPHER

> *Question:* What is the best thing to do in a hurry?
> *Answer:* Nothing.
> PUNCH MAGAZINE

Abolish fear and you can accomplish anything you wish.
DR CHARLES E. WELCH, OF WELCH'S GRAPE JUICE

In a moment of decision, the best thing you can do is the right thing to do. The worst thing you can do is nothing.
THEODORE ROOSEVELT, US PRESIDENT

The lure of the distant and difficult is deceptive. The greatest opportunity is where you are.
JOHN BURROUGHS, AMERICAN NATURALIST

When problems cease, so do opportunities. Solving problems was the reason you were hired. And it's been my experience that jobs with few problems don't pay very much.
H. JACKSON BROWN JR, MOTIVATIONAL AUTHOR

If the desire to write is not accompanied by actual writing, the desire is not to write.
HUGH PRATHER, WRITER

The greatest pleasure in life is doing what people say you cannot do.
WALTER BAGEHOT, BRITISH ECONOMIST AND JOURNALIST

> Opportunity's favourite disguise is trouble.
> FRANK TYGER

> Being bored is an insult to oneself.
> JULES RENARD, FRENCH WRITER

If you have a weakness, make it work for you as a strength — and if you have a strength, don't abuse it into a weakness.
DORE SCHARY, FILM PRODUCER, SCREENWRITER

There's a trick to the graceful exit. It begins with the vision to recognise when a job, a life stage, or a relationship is over and let it go. It means leaving what's over without denying its validity or its past importance to our lives. It involves a sense of future, a belief that every exit line is an entry, that we are moving on, rather than out.

ELLEN GOODMAN, JOURNALIST

People will never know how long it takes you to do something. They will only know how well it is done.

NANCY HANKS

Strength does not come from winning. Your struggles develop your strengths. When you go through hardships and decide not to surrender, that is strength.

ARNOLD SCHWARZENEGGER, BODYBUILDER AND ACTOR

To finish first you must first finish.
RICK MEARS, MOTOR RACING

It's hard to beat a person who never gives up.
BABE RUTH, BASEBALL

Success is living up to your potential. That's all. Wake up with a smile and go after life. Don't just show up at the game or office. Live it, enjoy it, taste it, smell it, feel it.

JOE KAPP, AMERICAN FOOTBALL

To hope is to risk pain. To try is to risk failure. But risk must be taken, because the greatest hazard in life is to risk nothing. The person who risks nothing does nothing, has nothing and is nothing. He may avoid suffering and sorrow, but he simply cannot learn, feel, change, grow, live or love. Chained by his additions, he's a slave. He has forfeited his greatest trait and that is his individual freedom. Only the person who risks is free.

LEO BUSCAGLIA, AMERICAN PSYCHOLOGIST AND WRITER

> Heart is what separates the good from the great
> MICHAEL JORDAN, BASKETBALL

> Spectacular achievements are always preceded by unspectacular preparation.
> ROGER STAUBACH, AMERICAN FOOTBALL

> If the love of what you're doing exceeds the labour of doing — success is inevitable.
> BOB BEERS

> Once you've been No. 1, you can never be satisfied with less.
> CHRIS EVERT, TENNIS

> Forewarned, forearmed; to be prepared is half the victory.
> MIGUEL DE CERVANTES, SPANISH NOVELIST

> Strong reasons make strong actions.
> WILLIAM SHAKESPEARE, ENGLISH PLAYWRIGHT AND POET

THERE ARE TWO TYPES OF STRENGTH:

There is the strength of the wind that sways the mighty oak, and there is the strength of the oak that withstands the power of the wind.

There is the strength of the locomotive that pulls the heavy train across the bridge, and there is the strength of the bridge that holds up the weight of the train.

One is active strength; the other is passive strength.

One is the power to keep going, the other is the power to keep still.

One is the strength by which we overcome, the other is the strength by which we endure.

Dr Harold Phillips

Success is not getting on top — it's how you bounce on the bottom that counts.

GENERAL GEORGE PATTON

Whatever your work, dignify it with your best thought and effort.

ESTHER BALDWIN YORK

No problem can withstand the assault of sustained thinking.

VOLTAIRE, FRENCH PHILOSOPHER AND WRITER

I've missed more than good shots in my career. I've lost almost 300 games. Twenty-six times I've been trusted to take the game-winning shot and missed. I've failed over and over again in my life. And that is why I succeed.

MICHAEL JORDAN, BASKETBALL

The best impromptu speeches are the ones written well in advance.

RUTH GORDON, US ACTRESS

I've got my faults but living in the past isn't one of them. There ain't no future in it.

SPARKY ANDERSON, BASEBALL

If you can react the same way to winning and losing, that is a big accomplishment. That quality is important because it stays with you the rest of your life.

CHRIS EVERT, TENNIS

Always aim for achievement and forget about success.

HELEN HAYES, US ACTRESS

It does not matter how slowly you go, so long as you do not stop.

CONFUCIUS, CHINESE TEACHER AND PHILOSOPHER

Difficulty is an excuse history never accepts.

EDWARD R. MURROW, AMERICAN JOURNALIST

Now if you are going to win any battle, you have to do one thing. You have to make the mind run the body. Never let the body tell the mind what to do. The body will always give up. It is always tired — morning, noon and night.

When you were younger, the mind could make you dance all night. You've always got to make the mind take over and keep going.

GENERAL GEORGE PATTON

I'm just a ballplayer with one ambition, and that is to give all I've got to help my club win. I've never played any other way.

JOE DIMAGGIO, BASEBALL

The harder the conflict, the more glorious the triumph. What we obtain too cheap, we esteem too lightly.

THOMAS PAINE, AMERICAN WRITER

I'm not out there sweating for three hours every day just to find out what it feels like to sweat.

MICHAEL JORDAN, BASKETBALL

Work banishes those three great evils: boredom, vice and poverty.

VOLTAIRE, FRENCH PHILOSOPHER AND WRITER

Good and quickly seldom meet.

GEORGE HERBERT, BRITISH CLERGYMAN AND POET

The best career advice given to the young is: 'Find out what you like doing best and get someone to pay you for doing it.'

KATHERINE WHITEHORN

If you don't do something, nothing is going to get better.

NATHANIEL BRANDEN, PROFESSIONAL THERAPIST AND AUTHOR

Accept the challenges, so that you may feel the exhilaration of victory.

GENERAL GEORGE PATTON

> Your future depends on many things, but mostly on you.
> FRANK TYGER

There are moments when everything goes well. Don't be frightened. It won't last.
JULES RENARD, FRENCH WRITER

> Sweat is the cologne of accomplishment.
> HEYWOOD C. BROUN, US JOURNALIST

The problem with doing nothing is not knowing when you're finished.
BENJAMIN FRANKLIN, US SCIENTIST AND DIPLOMAT

ONE MORE THING ...

P.S.: Knowledge without action is like snow on a hot stove.

P.S.: You'll never build a reputation, a business, or a relationship on what you intend to do. Your intentions may be honourable and sincere, but unless you put them into action, nothing is changed.

P.S.: The great man shows his greatness by the way he treats the little man.

P.S.: As you climb the ladder of success, be sure it's leaning against the right building.

P.S.: Luck is what happens when preparation meets opportunity.

P.S.: If you're doing your best, you won't have any time to worry about failure.

P.S.: So you wish that all the problems at work would go away. Maybe you'd better think again.

H. Jackson Brown Jr., motivational author. These are actually postscripts to letters written by Brown's mother to family members, featured in his book P.S. I Love You *(Rutledge Hill Press, 2000).*

The road to success is always under construction.
ARNOLD PALMER, GOLF

Life is not a spectator sport — if you're going to spend your whole life in the grandstand just watching what goes on, in my opinion you're wasting your life.
JACKIE ROBINSON, BASEBALL

The hardest work in the world is being out of work.
WHITNEY YOUNG, CIVIL RIGHTS ACTIVIST

Don't be afraid to give your best to what seemingly are small jobs. Every time you conquer one, it makes you feel that much stronger. If you do the little jobs well, the big jobs will take care of themselves.
DALE CARNEGIE, US WRITER

You miss 100 per cent of the shots you never take.
WAYNE GRETZKY, ICE HOCKEY

Success doesn't always go to the most experienced and talented. It generally goes to the most tenacious.
KEVIN SHEEDY, AUSTRALIAN FOOTBALL

Never give up on what you really want to do. The person with big dreams is more powerful than one with all the facts.
H. JACKSON BROWN JR, MOTIVATIONAL AUTHOR

The future comes one day at a time.
DEAN ACHESON, US LAWYER AND STATESMAN

Time is a created thing. To say, 'I don't have time', is like saying, 'I don't want to.'
LAO-TZU, CHINESE PHILOSOPHER AND TEACHER

It takes 20 years to make an overnight success.
EDDIE CANTOR, AMERICAN ENTERTAINER

When you have a great and difficult task, something perhaps almost impossible, if you only work a little at a time, every day a little, suddenly the work will finish itself.

ISAK DINESEN, DANISH WRITER

There is no happiness except in the realisation that we have accomplished something.

HENRY FORD, FOUNDER, FORD MOTOR COMPANY

Be kind, for everyone you meet is fighting a hard battle.

PLATO, GREEK PHILOSOPHER

The toughest thing about success is that you've got to keep on being a success.

IRVING BERLIN, US SONGWRITER

The thing that drives a real pro is simply inner satisfaction. That's all.

MERLIN OLSEN, AMERICAN FOOTBALL

If a question is important, be willing to invest in answering it.

KARL ALBRECHT, MANAGEMENT CONSULTANT

If every day was a constant struggle, it usually meant I was going in the wrong direction.

DOUG PETERSON

My theory has always been that if you want something, if you can see it, if you can visualise it, and you are willing to pay the price of very hard work, then you can achieve it.

HERB MCKENLEY, TRACK AND FIELD

ELEVEN

Human Nature

'Man is the only creature that must be coached.'

The deepest principle in human nature is the craving to be appreciated.
DALE CARNEGIE, US WRITER

A young psychology student serving in the Army decided to test a theory. Drawing kitchen duty, he was given the job of passing cut apricots at the end of the chow line. He asked the first few soldiers that came by, 'You don't want any apricots, do you?' Ninety per cent said no.

Then he tried the positive approach: 'You do want apricots, don't you?' About half answered, 'Uh, yeah, I'll take some.'

Then he tried a third test. This time he asked: 'One dish of apricots or two?' And in spite of the fact that soldiers don't like Army apricots, 40 per cent took two dishes and 50 per cent took one.

Deep within man dwell these slumbering powers that would astonish him, that he never dreamed of possessing; forces that would revolutionise his life if aroused and put into action.
ORISON SWETT MARDEN, AMERICAN MAGAZINE EDITOR

Advice to Writers
The worst words you ever write are better
than the best words you never write.

We have to learn to be our own best friends because we fall easily into the trap of being our own worst enemies.
RODERICK THORP, CRIME NOVELIST

We are always hard on our faults when we see them in others. Perhaps the reason is that we know how inexcusable they are.

All marriages are happy — it's living together afterwards that can be troublesome.
DR LAURENCE PETER, CANADIAN EDUCATOR

People can be divided into three groups:
1. Those who make things happen
2. Those who watch things happen, and
3. Those who wonder what's happening.

For every coach wishing to teach there are thirty not wanting to be taught.
W.C. SELLAR AND R.J. YEATMAN, HISTORY WRITERS

Don't worry about people stealing your ideas. If your ideas are any good, you'll have to ram them down people's throats.
HOWARD AIKEN, US COMPUTER SCIENTIST

The person who is worthy of being a coach will never complain of the stupidity of his helpers, of the ingratitude of mankind, or of the lack of appreciation of the public. These things are all a part of the great game of life, and to meet them and not go down before them in discouragement and defeat, is the final proof of power.
ELBERT GREEN HUBBARD, US BUSINESSMAN AND WRITER

> **ARE YOU A HUMBLE COACH?**
>
> Do you consider others in your organisation to be as important as you are?
>
> Do you respect their time as much as your own?
>
> Do you hold yourself to the same standards that you set for others?
>
> Are you genuinely interested in what lower-level employees have to say?
>
> Do employees at lower levels of your organisation approach you frequently and comfortably?
>
> Are you often uncomfortable receiving praise?
>
> Are you sometimes reluctant to make public statements or bold public action?
>
> Leader to Leader *Magazine*

Coaches must strive to embrace humility and charisma.

Charisma becomes the undoing of coaches. It makes them inflexible, convinced of their own infallibility, unable to change.
PETER F. DRUCKER, BUSINESS ANALYST, SOCIAL COMMENTATOR, AUTHOR

Charisma can win players over ... until results begin to slip.
PATRICK LENCIONI, MANAGEMENT CONSULTANT AND AUTHOR

Players need more than money to be happy. They also want a challenging job that brings a sense of achievement, responsibility, growth, advancement, enjoyment of work itself and recognition.

Fame is a vapour, popularity an accident, riches take wings. Only one thing endures, and that is character.
HORACE GREELING, NEWSPAPER EDITOR AND PUBLISHER

The pro is a person who can do his job when he doesn't feel like it. The amateurs are people who can't do their job when they do feel like it.

I have a very strong feeling that the opposite of love is not hate — it's apathy, it's not giving a damn.
LEO BUSCAGLIA, AMERICAN PSYCHOLOGIST AND WRITER

> Love looks through a telescope;
> Envy through a microscope.
> JOSH BILLINGS, HUMORIST

Character is the best way to obtain credit; it is also the best way to win the confidence of the audience.
JOHN PIERPONT MORGAN, US BANKER AND FINANCIER

> Always make the other person feel important.
> DALE CARNEGIE, US WRITER

My personal philosophy is quite simple: I am responsible for me and must oversee with great sensitivity the impact of what I say and/or do on others.
BARBARA JORDAN, US POLITICIAN

There's so much bad in the best of us, and so much good in the worst of us, that it doesn't behove any of us to talk about the rest of us.
ANONYMOUS

> It is better to give than to lend, and it costs about the same.
> SIR PHILIP GIBBS, ENGLISH JOURNALIST AND NOVELIST

Half the harm that is done in the world is due to people who want to feel important.
T.S. ELIOT, ENGLISH POET AND DRAMATIST

One of the best ways to measure people is how they behave when something free is offered.

ANN LANDERS, AMERICAN ADVICE COLUMNIST

People come in all different shapes, sizes and colours. And what makes them special isn't their physical appearance or the clothes they wear. It's their personal values, ideas and the way they choose to conduct their lives.

If you don't make an effort to reach out and find those qualities in people, someone who could have been a great friend or business relationship will be gone and out of your life before even having a chance to enter it.

BILL DANIELS

Love your enemies.
It will drive them nuts.
ELEANOR DOAN, BOOK EDITOR

The love of liberty is the love of others; the love of power is the love of ourselves.

WILLIAM HAZLITT, ENGLISH ESSAYIST

All you need to do is tell people they are no good 10 times a day, and very soon they will begin to believe it.

LIN YU-T'ANG, CHINESE WRITER

Anxiety is simply part of the condition of being human. If we were not anxious, we would never create anything.

WILLIAM BARRETT

Indecision is the thief of opportunity.
JIM ROHN, MOTIVATIONAL SPEAKER

We are reluctant to let go of the belief that if I am to care for something I must control it.

PETER BLOCK, US AUTHOR AND MANAGEMENT CONSULTANT

> Character is not made in a crisis — it is only exhibited.
> ROBERT FREEMAN

Those only are happy who have their minds fixed on some object other than their own happiness — on the happiness of others.
JOHN STUART MILL, BRITISH ECONOMIST AND PHILOSOPHER

When dealing with people, let us remember we are not dealing with creatures of logic. We are dealing with people of emotion, creatures bristling with prejudices and motivated by pride and vanity.
DALE CARNEGIE, US WRITER

When you can, advise people to do what they really want to do — doing what they want to do, they may succeed; doing what they don't want to do, they won't.
JAMES G. COZZENS, US WRITER

ARE YOU A CHARISMATIC COACH?

Do you consider your actions to be more important than those of the other people in your organisation?

Do you look for opportunities to make public statements or take bold public action?

Are you aware of the extent that you actively manage your actions for public effect?

Do people tell you they enjoy hearing you speak?

Are people in your organisation hesitant to give you frank and honest feedback? Are you sure?

Do you believe that your personal leadership is the key to your organisation's success?

Are you comfortable receiving praise?

Leader to Leader *Magazine*

TWELVE

Forks in the Road

'Strength comes to the coach who dares.'

Baseball can teach you to never let the fear of striking out get in your way.

BABE RUTH, BASEBALL

Whatever we learn to do, we learn by actually doing it; men come to be builders, for instance, by building and harp players by playing the harp. In the same way, by doing just acts, we come to be just; by doing self-controlled acts, we come to be self-controlled and by doing brave acts, we become brave.

ARISTOTLE, GREEK SCIENTIST AND PHILOSOPHER

Everyday courage has few witnesses. But yours is no less noble because no drum beats before you and no crowds shout your name.

ROBERT LOUIS STEVENSON, SCOTTISH AUTHOR

Failure should be our teacher, not our undertaker. Failure is delay, not defeat. It is a temporary detour not a dead-end street.

BITS & PIECES MAGAZINE

Successful coaches find ways to cope with their fears of the unknown.
> WILLIAM E. FULMER, TEACHER AND BUSINESS WRITER

When you come to a fork in the road, take it.
> YOGI BERRA, BASEBALL

The hero and the coward both feel the same thing, but the hero uses his fear, projects it onto his opponent, while the coward runs. It's the same thing, fear, but it's what you do with it that matters.
> CUS D'AMATO, BOXING TRAINER

Our fears are always more numerous than our dangers.
> SENECA, ROMAN STATESMAN AND TEACHER

Always do what you are afraid to do.
> RALPH WALDO EMERSON, US ESSAYIST AND POET

A coach who carries a grudge falls behind.

Changing one small thing for the better is worth more than proving a thousand people wrong.
> ANTHONY PIVEC

Ignore the ones who say it's too late to start over. Disregard those who say you'll never amount to anything. Turn a deaf ear to those who say you aren't smart enough, fast enough, tall enough, or big enough — ignore them.
> MAX LUCADO, THEOLOGIAN AND AUTHOR

The more we cling to past practices, the more we deepen the crisis and prevent solutions.
> MARGARET WHEATLEY, AUTHOR, MANAGEMENT CONSULTANT

The golden opportunity you are seeking is in yourself. It is not in your environment; it is not in luck or chance, or the help of others; it is in yourself alone.

ORISON SWETT MARDEN,
AMERICAN MAGAZINE EDITOR

Here is a test to find whether your mission on earth is finished; if you're alive, it isn't.

RICHARD BACH, AUTHOR

When I told my father I was going to be an actor, he said, 'Fine, but study welding — just in case.'

ROBIN WILLIAMS, US COMEDIAN AND ACTOR

You can only have two things in life, reasons or results. Reasons don't count.

ROBERT ANTHONY, PSYCHOLOGIST AND MOTIVATOR

If there's no struggle, there is no progress.

FREDERICK DOUGLASS, AMERICAN ABOLITIONIST AND WRITER

It takes the same amount of courage to have tried and failed as it does to have tried and succeeded.

ANNE MORROW LINDBERGH, AMERICAN WRITER, PILOT

You are what you are when nobody is looking.

ABIGAIL VAN BUREN, US COLUMNIST

You can do something about yesterday tomorrow.

MANNY TRILLO, BASEBALL

In football, people remember you for your hits — while the misses fade into obscurity.

WAYNE ALLYN ROOT, US SPORTS ANALYST, MOTIVATOR, TV PERSONALITY

All glory comes from daring to begin.

EUGENE F. WARE, WRITER AND EDUCATOR

IN THE WORDS OF YOGI ...

Few sportspeople can match Yogi Berra, 10-time World Series winning catcher with the New York Yankees and later a highly successful Major League manager, when it comes to getting their words twisted while often still being perceptive. The baseball encyclopedia, Total Baseball, *calls Berra (real name Lawrence Peter Berra) 'the most quoted person in baseball history'. Berra himself comments: 'I really didn't say everything I said.' Here are a handful of well-known 'Yogi-isms' ...*

'You can observe a lot just by watching.'

'He must have made that before he died.'
(Referring to a Steve McQueen movie.)

'It ain't over till it's over.'

'If you don't know where you're going, you won't know when you get there.'

'Yeah, but we're making great time!'
(In reply to his passenger, teammate Phil Rizzuto, saying, 'Hey, Yogi, I think we're lost.')

Make it a point to do something every day that you don't want to do. This is the golden rule for acquiring the habit of doing your duty without pain.

MARK TWAIN, US WRITER

Courage is what it takes to stand up and speak.
Courage is also what it takes to sit down and listen.

SIR WINSTON CHURCHILL, BRITISH PRIME MINISTER

> 'You've got to be very careful if you don't know where you're going, because you might not get there.'
>
> 'If you can't imitate him, don't copy him.'
>
> 'Baseball is 90-per-cent mental — the other half is physical.'
>
> 'How long have you known me, Jack? And you still don't know how to spell my name.'
> *(After receiving a cheque from the legendary baseball commentator Jack Buck made out to 'bearer'.)*
>
> 'It was impossible to get a conversation going; everybody was talking too much.'
>
> 'Slump? I ain't in no slump. I just ain't hitting.'
>
> 'Do you mean now?'
> *(When asked for the time.)*
>
> 'I take a two-hour nap, from one o'clock to four.'
>
> 'We made too many wrong mistakes.'
> *(Explaining why the Yankees lost the 1960 World Series to Pittsburgh.)*
>
> 'The other teams could make trouble for us if they win.'

In the middle of difficulty lies opportunity.
ALBERT EINSTEIN, PHYSICIST

The pro is the person who has all of the hassles, obstacles and disappointing frustrations that everyone else has — yet continues to persist, does the job and makes it look easy.

DAVID COOPER, FINANCIAL TRAINER
AND MOTIVATIONAL SPEAKER

Never be afraid to stand with the minority when the minority is right, for the minority that is right will one day be the majority. Always be afraid to stand with the majority that is wrong, for the majority that is wrong will one day be the minority.

WILLIAM JENNINGS BRYAN, US SECRETARY OF STATE

When you win, nothing hurts.

JOE NAMATH, AMERICAN FOOTBALL

Fear is a very natural and normal response to the challenges we face in life. Fear tells us there is something we must be cautious about. Fear puts us on alert and tells us there is something we must be prepared for. Fear means something we know nothing about is to come upon us. Fear of change, the unknown, rejection, failure and success are like the barking of a ferocious bulldog.

IYANLA VANZANT, AUTHOR AND PUBLIC SPEAKER

The trouble is, if you don't risk anything, you risk even more.

ERICA JONG, NOVELIST

Fear is your best friend or your worst enemy. It's like fire. If you can control it, it can cook for you; it can heat your house. If you can't control it, it will burn everything around you and destroy you.

CUS D'AMATO, BOXING TRAINER

The unexpected always happens.

DR LAURENCE PETER, CANADIAN EDUCATOR

Courage faces fear and thereby masters it.

MARTIN LUTHER KING JNR, CIVIL RIGHTS ACTIVIST

Nobody trips over mountains. It is the small pebble that causes you to stumble. Pass all the pebbles in your path and you will find you have crossed the mountain.

ANONYMOUS

The greatest test of courage on earth is to bear defeat without losing heart.
>
> ROBERT GREEN INGERSOLL, ORATOR

You are only courageous when you do what you feel is right despite your fear. Everyone feels fear, so everyone can be courageous.
>
> TOM RUSK, FROM *GET OUT OF YOUR OWN WAY!* (HAY HOUSE, INC., 1996)

Some of us are timid. We think we have something to lose so we don't try for the next hill.
>
> MAYA ANGELOU, AMERICAN ACTRESS AND AUTHOR

Any change, even a change for the better, is always accompanied by drawbacks and discomforts.
>
> ARNOLD BENNETT, BRITISH NOVELIST AND ESSAYIST

To keep from decaying, to be a winner, the athlete must accept pain — not only accept it, but look for it, live with it, learn not to fear it.
>
> DR GEORGE SHEEHAN, RUNNER, CARDIOLOGIST, AUTHOR, PHILOSOPHER

To give without any reward, or any notice, has a special quality of its own.
>
> ANNE MORROW LINDBERGH, AMERICAN WRITER, PILOT

Only a mediocre person is always at their best.
>
> W. SOMERSET MAUGHAM, ENGLISH NOVELIST AND DRAMATIST

How to do something extraordinary ...
Stage 1: First it will seem impossible.
Stage 2: Then it will become difficult.
Stage 3: Finally, with persistence, it will get done.

THIRTEEN

Face the Music

'Opportunity doesn't come, it's here!'

The fight is won far away from witnesses — behind the lines, in the gym, and out there on the road — long before I dance under those lights.

MUHAMMAD ALI, WORLD HEAVYWEIGHT BOXING CHAMPION

Once you learn how good you really are, you never settle for playing less than your best.

REGGIE JACKSON, BASEBALL

Obviously, people must have knowledge in their fields. But the greatest success and financial reward will go to the coach who has more; the ability to press their ideas to assume leadership, to arouse enthusiasm and co-operation. In short, the ability to bring out the best in others.

Never rest on your oars as a coach. If you do, the whole team starts sinking.

LEE IACOCCA, BUSINESS EXECUTIVE

In football and other sports, as well as business, the good athletes are hard to find. Needless failures are costly. If there is anything that might be done to help a new player succeed, it's worth the time and effort of everyone.

FRAN TARKENTON, AMERICAN FOOTBALL

Real coaches face the music, even if they don't like the tune.

Coaching is a progressive course, not an end to be reached.

Conditions are never just right. Coaches who delay action until all factors are favourable do nothing.

WILLIAM FEATHER, US PUBLISHER, AUTHOR

On the road to success, you may be sure of one thing — there is never a crowd on the extra mile.

ANONYMOUS

THE KEY PEOPLE

WANTED: players for hard work, players who can find things to be done without the help of a coach and three assistants. Players who get to training on time and do not imperil the lives of others in an attempt to be first to leave training each session; players who listen carefully when they are spoken to and ask only enough questions to ensure the accurate carrying out of instructions; players who look you straight in the eye and tell the truth every time; players who do not sulk about extra training in emergencies; players who are cheerful and courteous to everyone, and determined to make good. These players are wanted everywhere. Age or lack of experience does not count. There isn't any limit, except their own ambitions, to the number or size of the jobs they can get. They are wanted in every business.

The coach who is anybody and who does anything is going to be criticised, vilified and misunderstood. That is part of the penalty for greatness and every man understands it and understands, too, that it is no proof of greatness. The final proof of greatness lies in being able to endure continuously without resentment.
ELBERT GREEN HUBBARD, US BUSINESSMAN AND WRITER

It's never too late to be what you might have been.
GEORGE ELIOT, ENGLISH NOVELIST

When you get to the top, regardless of your field — business, politics, sport, entertainment or whatever — you are bound to be criticised. It's easy to find fault. That's why so many people do it.

Don't agonise, organise.
FLORYNCE KENNEDY, LAWYER AND POLITICAL ACTIVIST

There are no secrets to success. Don't waste time looking for them. Success is the result of perfection, hard work, learning from failure, loyalty to those for whom you work and persistence.
COLIN POWELL, US SECRETARY OF STATE

THE BATTLE CONTINUES

When victory is achieved, that feeling can be overwhelming.

Keep your commonsense about you, and be gracious.

Silence is often the best tactic after a win.

Decide what you want.

Decide what you are willing to exchange for it.

Establish your priorities.

Go to work.

H.L. Hunt, oil tycoon

Example is not the main thing in influencing others; it is the only thing.
ALBERT SCHWEITZER, THEOLOGIAN
AND NOBEL PEACE PRIZE WINNER

Success is to be measured not so much by the position that one has reached in life as by the obstacles one has overcome while trying to succeed.
BOOKER T. WASHINGTON, US EDUCATOR, WRITER

It ain't bragging if you can do it.
DIZZY DEAN, BASEBALL

All I have is enthusiasm and drive.
BETTE MIDLER, SINGER AND ACTRESS

Wanting something is not enough. You must hunger for it. Your motivation must be absolutely compelling in order to overcome the obstacles than invariably come your way.
LES BROWN, MOTIVATIONAL SPEAKER

There are no victories at bargain prices.
DWIGHT EISENHOWER, US PRESIDENT

You always pass failure on the way to success.
MICKEY ROONEY, ACTOR

What I have learned is there ain't no genie. I am it. If the wealth and adventure and fame are to come, I'd better get tough on the only one who can make it happen — me.
TY BOYD, BUSINESS CONSULTANT

My life is one big obstacle course, with me being the chief obstacle.
JACK PAAR, TV AND RADIO PERSONALITY

It is better to look ahead and prepare than to look back and regret.

JACKIE JOYNER-KERSEE, TRACK AND FIELD

I never tried quitting and I never quit trying.

DOLLY PARTON, SINGER AND ACTRESS

When faced with a decision — DECIDE.
When faced with a choice — CHOOSE.
Sitting on the fence will leave you tense,
Because you neither win nor lose!

BARRY SPILCHUK, SPEAKER, TRAINER AND AUTHOR

It's the quality of the time you spend practicing that counts — not the length of time.

JIMMY CONNORS, TENNIS

TO BE THE BEST

I've watched many people in various lines of endeavour striving to attain the best and I have tried to determine what qualities they had in common.

Whether they were baseball pitchers trying for a no-hit game, sprinters attempting to break a world record, or grape growers intent on producing the finest wine in the world, they all had complete dedication to their goals.

They displayed greater knowledge than their competitors; they were willing to put in the extra effort necessary to approach perfection; they never settled for second best. They exerted themselves to reach these heights of accomplishment for both financial rewards and esteem of their peers or clients, and for their own satisfaction.

Stanley Marcus, US retailer

If winning has become too important, it might be time to question whether the ends justify the means. They usually don't.
JOHN L. BECKLEY, PUBLISHER

Along the way you will stumble and perhaps even fall; but that, too is normal and to be expected. Get up, get back on your feet, chastened but wiser, and continue on down the road.
ARTHUR ASHE, TENNIS

Measure twice. Saw once.
CARPENTERS' MAXIM

Greatness occurs when your children love you, when your critics respect you, and when you have peace of mind.
DR DENNIS P. KIMBRO, AUTHOR, EDUCATOR

FOURTEEN

The Art of Coaching

'Effective coaches know when to do what with whom.'

The superior coach gets things done with little motion. He imparts instructions not through many words, but through a few deeds. He keeps informed about everything, but interferes hardly at all. He is a catalyst, and though things would not get done as well if he weren't there, when they succeed, he takes no credit. And because he takes no credit, credit never leaves him.

LAO-TZU, CHINESE PHILOSOPHER

No man will make a coach who wants to do it all himself, or to get all the credit for doing it.

ANDREW CARNEGIE, US STEEL MAGNATE

People will sit up and take notice of you if you will sit up and take notice of what makes them sit up and take notice.

FRANK ROMER

The best coach is not the one who crams the most into the pupil, but the one who gets the most out of him.

SYDNEY J. HARRIS, SYNDICATED COLUMNIST

To know how to do a job is the accomplishment of labour,
To be available to tell others is the accomplishment of the teacher,
To inspire others to do better work is the accomplishment of management,
To be able to do all three is the accomplishment of COACHING.

The task of the coach is to get his players from where they are to where they have not been.
HENRY KISSINGER, US SECRETARY OF STATE

The good coach is not the person who does things right, but the one who finds the right things to do.

If you're the coach and your people fight you openly when they think you are wrong, that's healthy. If your people fight each other openly in your presence for what they believe in, that's healthy.
ROBERT TOWNSEND

You can judge coaches by the size of the problems they tackle — people nearly always pick a problem their own size, and ignore or leave to others the bigger or smaller ones.
ANTHONY JAY

The most important signal management can send is to empower the players to make decisions. Let those on the field play the game. Don't let rules and policies outweigh suggestions.

The wicked coach is he whom the players despise. The good coach is he whom the players revere. The great coach is he whom the players say, 'We did it ourselves.'
LAO-TZU, CHINESE PHILOSOPHER

The coach's worst decision is the one that is never made
BYRD BAGGETT, MOTIVATIONAL SPEAKER

The coach of a highly rated football club was asked the secret of his success. 'It's really very simple,' he said. 'I always apply the rule of the 3 Ds: Do it, Delegate it, or Ditch it.'

> Flatter me and I may not believe you.
> Criticise me and I may not like you.
> Ignore me and I may not forgive you.
> Encourage me and I will not forget you.
> WILLIAM ARTHUR WARD, US AUTHOR AND SCHOLAR

When you get a coach's job, surround yourself with the best people you can find, delegate authority and don't interfere.

Coaches who enjoy responsibility usually get it; those who merely like exercising authority usually lose it.
MALCOLM FORBES, AMERICAN BILLIONAIRE

HOW TO MAKE YOURSELF A MORE LIKEABLE COACH

1. Be considerate — make listeners comfortable.
2. Get off to a good start — be strong and warm.
3. Choose your words carefully, so they can understand.
4. Persuade — request work rather than order.
5. Relate — don't hide behind a deadpan look.
6. Be patient — people think at different speeds.
7. Some people have personal problems.
8. Admit your weaknesses — pay compliments.
9. Express thanks.
10. Finally, consider Lord Chesterfield's advice: 'Be wiser than other people, if you can, but do not tell them so.'

Roger Ailes, media executive

The coach can spend a lifetime assigning blame, finding a cause 'out there' for all troubles that exist. Contrast this with the 'responsible attitude' of confronting the situation, bad or good, and instead of asking, 'What caused the trouble? Who was to blame?', asking: 'How can I handle this present situation to make the best of it?'

ABRAHAM MASLOW, PSYCHOLOGIST, AUTHOR

Great coaches never set themselves above their followers except in carrying responsibilities.

JULES ORMONT, MOTIVATIONAL SPEAKER

A coach should know more than he coaches, and if he knows more than he coaches, he will coach more than he knows.

Snap decisions can be unfortunate. On the other hand, there are times when you must pick up the dice and throw them; when, regardless of whether you have all the facts or not, a decision has to be made. In a situation like this, you've got to weigh the risks.

What important facts are missing and how long would it take to get them? Is a prompt decision so important you can't wait for the necessary information?

When you've thought it all over, make your decision and don't look back.

JOHN L. BECKLEY, PUBLISHER

The most important thing for a coach is to remain stable under all that pressure.

> The difference between coaches and managers ...
> Managers have as their goal to do things right;
> Coaches have as their goal to do the right thing.
>
> PROFESSOR WARREN BENNIS

The first rule of cleaning out a cluttered office or closet: when in doubt, throw it out.

Coaching cannot really be taught. It can only be learned.
HAROLD S. GENEEN, BUSINESS EXECUTIVE

The ability to foretell what will happen tomorrow, next month, and next year — and explain afterward why it didn't happen.
SIR WINSTON CHURCHILL, AFTER BEING ASKED TO NAME THE CHIEF QUALIFICATION REQUIRED BY A COACH

People ask the difference
between a coach and a boss.
The coach works in the open
and the boss in covert.
The coach leads and the boss drives.
THEODORE ROOSEVELT, US PRESIDENT

WHEN TO WORRY

I was just 16, five foot three, 120lbs, and playing junior varsity football. For the first few weeks of practice, my coach, George Herrick, continually seemed to pick on me: 'You missed your assignment! Hit that hole harder!' And so on. One day, I snapped and yelled back at him. He kicked me out of practice. But later I apologised and he said something that I've used ever since — in business, in coaching, little League, and even with my kids: 'Don't worry when the coach yells at you — worry when he stops.' I just didn't realise that he saw something in me and cared enough to help. By the way, I rejoined the team and made first string.

Ronald Gross, motivator and author

Reputation is what you have when you come to a new community. Character is what you have when you go away.

WILLIAM H. DAVIS

The great secret of successful coaching is to treat all disasters as incidents and none of the incidents as disasters.

SIR HAROLD NICOLSON, BRITISH DIPLOMAT AND WRITER

The greatest lesson a coach can teach is that life is a process, not an event.

JOHNNETTA B. COLE, EDUCATOR AND WRITER

Most coaches have enough problems to command their attention and use up their time. But it's a mistake to let these problems distract you from the most important job of all — keeping the players who play for you interested and inspired, and in a mood to do their best.

To feel this way and keep feeling it, players need personal attention and interest from the coach today and tomorrow — it's not something you can do every six months and forget about it in between.

Being in politics is like being a football coach; you have to be smart enough to understand the game, and dumb enough to think it's important.

EUGENE McCARTHY, US POLITICIAN

The first and last task of a coach is to keep hope alive.

JOHN W. GARDNER, US ADMINISTRATOR AND AUTHOR

Coaching is a word and a concept that has been more argued than almost any other I know. I am not one of the desk pounding types that likes to stick out his jaw and look like he is bossing the show. I would far rather get behind and, recognising the frailties and the requirements of human nature, would rather try to persuade a man to go along, because once I have persuaded him, he will stick. If I scare him, he will stay just as long as he is scared and then he is gone.

DWIGHT EISENHOWER, US PRESIDENT

The best test of whether someone is a qualified coach is to find out whether anyone is following him.

J. OSWALD SANDERS, RELIGIOUS WRITER

You don't have to be brilliant to be a good coach. But you do have to understand other people — how they feel, what makes them tick, the best way to influence them.

JOHN L. BECKLEY, PUBLISHER

The poor coach makes the interested student less interested. The good coach makes the interested student more interested. The superior coach makes the uninterested student interested.

ROB GILBERT, EDITOR, *BITS & PIECES*

Reason and judgment are the qualities of a coach.

TACITUS, ROMAN HISTORIAN

Now you're coach, the first principle is that you must not fool yourself — and you are the easiest person to fool.

RICHARD P. FEYNMAN, US PHYSICIST

The test of a good coach is not how many questions he can ask his players that they will answer readily, but how many questions he inspires them to ask him which he finds it hard to answer.

ALICE WELLINGTON ROLLINS, US WRITER AND POET

The best coaches are those who are willing to suffer the most over their decisions but still retain their ability to be decisive.

M. SCOTT PECK, PSYCHIATRIST AND WRITER

The team that makes the most mistakes will probably win. The doer makes mistakes. Mistakes come from doing, but so does success.

PIGGY LAMBERT, BASKETBALL

Coaching is …
- Knowing what to do next;
- Knowing why it's important;
- Knowing how to bring appropriate resources to bear on the need at hand.

BOB BIEHL

Does your coaching style tend to emphasise praise or criticism? It pays, every once in a while, to take a good look at yourself and be sure. And even when it's necessary to be critical of anyone, try to think of something they've done well. Praise first, then criticise if you must. Make it a habit.

JOHN L. BECKLEY, PUBLISHER

Coaching is the ability to reduce the complicated to the simple.

C.W. CERAR

Good coaches make their players think they have more ability than they have, so they consistently do better work than they thought they could.

CHARLES E. WILSON

As a coach, the important thing is not what happens when you are there, but what happens when you are not there.

KENNETH BLANCHARD, BUSINESS AUTHOR

The final test of a coach is that he leaves behind in others the conviction and will to carry on. The genius of a good coach is to leave behind a situation which commonsense, without the grace of genius, can deal with successfully.

WALTER LIPPMANN, US JOURNALIST AND AUTHOR

There'll be two buses leaving the hotel for the ball park tomorrow. The two o'clock bus will be for those of you who need a little extra work. The empty bus will be leaving at five o'clock.

DAVE BRISTOL, BASEBALL

The coach has to be practical and a realist, yet must talk the language of the visionary and the idealist.

ERIC HOFFER, AMERICAN PHILOSOPHER

The coach also has to surround himself with a strong people — not just lookalike clones but people who can make up for his or her shortcomings. And the coach has to build an environment that is not only fast, focused, flexible and friendly — but fun.

The secret of a coach lies in the tests he has faced over the whole course of his life and the habit of action he develops in meeting those tests.

GAIL SHEEHY, US AUTHOR AND JOURNALIST

Be yourself. Figure out what you're good at. Hire only good people who care. Treat them as the way you want to be treated. Switch from macro to maestro. Identify your one or two key objectives or directions. Ask your co-workers how to get there. Listen hard. Get out of their way. Cheer them. Count the gains. Start right now.

PROFESSOR WARREN BENNIS

Superior coaches get things done with very little motion. They impart instruction not through many words, but through a few deeds. They keep informed about everything but interfere hardly at all. They are catalysts. And because they take no credit, credit never leaves them.

LAO-TZU, CHINESE PHILOSOPHER

Successful coaches have self-confidence, vision, guts, and when necessary, they are not averse to relying on impulse. They have learned from everything, but they have learned more from experience, and even more from adversity and mistakes. They have learned to lead by leading.

PROFESSOR WARREN BENNIS

Coaches who don't look for co-operation first, sometimes don't really want it.

Friendly praise is such an effective coaching tool it's amazing that people don't use it more often. Take a look at somebody you consider an effective and pleasant coach. Have you ever bothered to notice how generous he or she is with praise and appreciation? The human appetite for praise is prodigious. No matter how much we got yesterday, we can always stand more today.

JOHN L. BECKLEY, PUBLISHER

Coaching is a state of mind and a way of life, not something that one turns on or off.

True coaches are always in the minority because they are thinking ahead of the majority. Even when the majority catches up, these coaches, or other coaches, will have moved ahead and so, again, will be in the minority.

HARRY MCKOWN, EDUCATOR AND WRITER

Coaching is like a book with many different chapters. Some tell of tragedy, others of triumph. Some chapters are dull and ordinary, others intense and exciting.

The key to being a success in life is to never stop on a tough chapter. Champions have the courage to keep turning the page because they know a better chapter lies ahead.

RICH RUFFALO, BLIND TRACK AND FIELD ATHLETE,
MOTIVATOR AND AUTHOR

The word 'influence' is the best one-word definition of coaching. Coaches are people who influence others to think, feel, or act in certain ways.

HANS FINZEL, RELIGIOUS AUTHOR

A competent coach can get efficient service from ordinary players, while on the contrary an incapable coach can demoralise the best of players.

GENERAL JOHN PERSHING

The best coaches are those most interested in surrounding themselves with assistants and associates smarter than they are.

AMOS PARRISH

The job of coaching today is not just to make money. It's to make meaning.

JOHN SEELY BROWN, SCIENTIST AND BUSINESS CONSULTANT

Good coaches grow people, bad coaches stunt them; good coaches serve their followers, bad coaches enslave them.

SIR ADRIAN CADBURY, COMPANY DIRECTOR
AND UNIVERSITY CHANCELLOR

The virtue of the coach ought to be measured not by his extraordinary exertions but by his everyday conduct.

PASCAL, FRENCH MATHEMATICIAN AND PHILOSOPHER

He that would coach others, first should be master of himself.

PHILIP MASSINGER, BRITISH DRAMATIST

It is a great pity when the one who should be the head coach is a mere figurehead.

C.H. SPURGEON, BRITISH PREACHER

Coaching is the ability to hide your panic from others.

When the coach blames others, he gives up his power to change.

ROBERT ANTHONY, PSYCHOLOGIST AND MOTIVATOR

> ### THE TOP TEN
>
> *In four years of executive seminars conducted by Santa Clara University and the Tom Peters Group/Learning Systems, more than 5200 senior managers were asked to describe the characteristics they most admire in a coach. Here are the top characteristics, as reported in* Management Review Magazine.
>
> | | |
> |---|---|
> | 1. Honest | 6. Fair-minded |
> | 2. Competent | 7. Broadminded |
> | 3. Forward-looking | 8. Courageous |
> | 4. Inspiring | 9. Straightforward |
> | 5. Intelligent | 10. Imaginative |
>
> Secrets of Executive Success *(Rodale Press, 1991)*

The final test of a coach is that he leaves behind him in other men the conviction and the will to carry on.

WALTER LIPPMANN, US JOURNALIST AND AUTHOR

When you make coach, do what needs to be done, but do it in a way that demonstrates you care how your action affects others.

LLOYD SMIGEL, MANAGEMENT CONSULTANT

The essence of coaching is getting your people to become what you know they can become.

MICKI HOLLIDAY, AUTHOR

Being a coach means playing off people's strengths instead of reprimanding them about their weaknesses.

GERALD CHAMALES, ENTREPRENEUR

Players hesitate in the presence of an unbalanced coach. People follow a coach in balance.

JOHN HETTERICK, BUSINESS EXECUTIVE

Good coaching should do more than attract followers. It should produce more coaches.

The true test of coaching is not the accolades you receive. It's what happens after you leave.
BERNARD TAYLOR, AUTHOR

Coaches should find ways — sometimes with humour — to remind players that the enemy is outside; it is not each other.

Good coaches inspire people to have confidence in them. Great coaches inspire people to have confidence in themselves.
SAM EWING, US HUMORIST

A good coach is someone who can understand those not very good at explaining and explain it to those who are not very good at understanding.

Code of Ethics
The welfare of the game depends on how the coaches live up to the spirit and letter of ethical conduct and remain ever mindful of the high trust placed in them by the players and the public.
THE AMERICAN COACHES ASSOCIATION

FIFTEEN

Proverbs

'There's always free cheese in a mousetrap.'

From China ...

One moment of patience may ward off a great disaster; one moment of impatience may ruin a whole career.

If you suspect a man, don't play him; if you play a man, don't suspect him.

A coach without followers is just a person going for a walk.

Coaches open the door, but you must enter by yourself.

An army of thousands is easy to find, but, ah, how difficult to find a general.

Great coaches have wills; feeble ones have only wishes.

It is the beautiful bird that we put in the cage.

From England ...
Deal with the faults of others as gently as with your own.

Only the wearer knows where a shoe pinches.

Do not climb the hill until you get to it.

From India ...
A man who cannot tolerate small ills can never accomplish great things.

You already possess everything necessary to become great.

The cobra will bite you whether you call it cobra or Mr Cobra.

From Spain ...
It takes two to quarrel, but only one to end it.

It's not the same to talk of bulls as to be in the bullring.

An Arab proverb ...
Only speak when your words are better than your silence.

Examine what is said, not the one who speaks.

From Denmark ...
Give to a pig when it grunts and a child when it cries, and you will have a fine pig and a bad child.

From Sweden ...
In calm waters, every ship has a good captain.

A Native American proverb ...
Show me and I may not remember.
Involve me and I'll understand.

From Germany
Fear makes the wolf bigger than he is.

From Turkey ...
Two captains sink a ship.

A Yiddish proverb ...
He that can't endure the bad will not live to see the good.

A Latin proverb ...
By learning you will teach; by coaching you will lead.

From Africa ...
It's on the path you do not fear that the wild beast catches you.

From Ireland ...
To the unwilling, nothing is easy.

From Italy ...
The best armour is to keep out of range.

From Baseball ...
It takes a whole season to win the Series.

SIXTEEN

Food for Thought

'When all else is lost the future still remains.'

The wisdom of life is to endure what we must and change what we can.

Failure is not the crime — low aim is.

If you don't have a plan for yourself, you'll be part of someone else's.

A team without goals is just another ineffective committee

Never let an individual dominate a team.

Praise does wonders for the sense of hearing.

The coach should remember when talking to the press that they always have the last word

Enjoy friends like flowers, but never cut them.

Courage is what it takes to stand up and speak; courage is also what it takes to sit down and listen.

Never let your authority blind you to the need for leadership.

Make no judgments where you have no compassion.

Some coaches call passing the buck delegating authority.

You have to serve many apprenticeships throughout your life. Show me someone who won't serve an apprenticeship, and I'll show you someone who won't go very far.

The street to obscurity is paved with athletes who performed great feats before friendly crowds. Greatness in major league sport is the ability to win in a stadium filled with people who are pulling for you to lose.

The player should be more concerned with his character than his reputation, because his character is what he really is, while his reputation is merely what others think he is.

The coach knows that the sportswriter is going to tip his team — either to win or lose. He may draw some comfort from the fact that there are two classes of forecasters: those who don't know and those who don't know they don't know.

Time to relax is when you don't have the time for it.

An ounce of practice is worth a pound of theory.

To err is human. To blame it on someone else is even more human.

Barking dogs seldom bite.

Do the hard jobs first. The easy ones will take care of themselves.

The only way to make players trustworthy is to trust them.

Second-rate people hire third-rate people.

A major advantage of age is learning to accept people.

There is nothing that fails like success.

With time and patience, the mulberry leaf becomes silk.

When you talk to people about themselves they are never bored.

There is less to fear from outside competition than from inside inefficiency, discourtesy and bad service.

Don't assume that spending twice as much will be twice as satisfying.

In a real contest, the greatest heroes are often found among the most ordinary players.

Nothing is easy but it becomes difficult when done reluctantly.

Some temptations come to the industrious, but all temptations come to the idle.

Those who are at war with others are not at peace with themselves.

The player who is sorry for himself is already half beaten.

Winning teams are not captained or coached by pessimists.

A good memory is one trained to forget the trivial.

> **TOMORROW**
>
> They were going to be all that they wanted to be — tomorrow.
>
> None would be braver, or kinder than they — tomorrow.
>
> A friend who was troubled and weary, they knew, would be glad of a lift — and needed it too.
>
> On him they would call — see what they could do — tomorrow.
>
> Each morning they stacked up the letters they'd write — tomorrow.
>
> The greatest of people they just might have been, the world would have opened its heart to them. But in fact, they passed on and faded from view, and all that they left when their living was through was a mountain of things they intended to do — tomorrow.

Agreeing to a thing in principle only means that you have no intention at all of carrying it out.

Only those who see the invisible can do the impossible.

Bad officials are elected by good citizens who do not vote.

He that falls in love with himself will have no rivals.

The most dangerous moment comes with victory.

Nothing is more costly, nothing is more sterile, than vengeance.

One makes no friends, who never made a foe.

Our lives would run a lot more smoothly if second thoughts came first.

Any person who can make hard things easier is a coach.

Win without boasting, lose without excuse.

Mind your own business and you'll never have time to be jealous.

You are not only responsible for what you do, but for what you don't do.

When you can look at yesterday without regret and at tomorrow without fear, you're on your way to the good life.

Success rarely comes to anyone, usually you have to go out and get it.

Opportunity always looks bigger going than coming.

We are all self-made, but only the rich will admit it.

Criticism never built a house, wrote a play, painted a picture, nor built a business.

Rust ruins more tools than overuse.

An artist is anyone who takes pride in doing a job well.

If you really want to do something you'll find a way; if you don't, you'll find an excuse.

You're never as old as you're going to get.

Every patient is a doctor after the cure.

A loafer is a person who is trying to make both weekends meet.

Do you remember who gave you your first break?

Going slow does not prevent arriving.

No one ever drowned in sweat.

If you only do what you are paid for, you'll never get paid for any more than you're currently doing.

Alter your attitude and you can alter your life.

Don't see all you see and don't hear all you hear.

It's the start that stops most people.

If you master patience, you may master everything else.

Fifty years ago, people finished a day's work and needed rest — today they need exercise.

There is a difference between wanting to get a good salary and wanting to earn a good salary.

We are all hypnotised by our fears and frustrations, because they become a habit.

Too many people are ready to carry the stool when a piano is to be moved.

Good coaches take a little more than their share of the blame and a little less than their share of the credit.

Be yourself — no one else is qualified.

A conference is a meeting at which people talk about things they should be doing.

If you keep doing what you've always done, you'll keep getting what you've always got.

If your mind should go blank, don't forget to turn off the sound.

The speed of the pack is determined by the speed of the leader.

The world stands aside to let those pass who know where they are going.

On someone else you can see a flea. On yourself you can't see an elephant.

Don't do for others what they can do for themselves.

If you want long friendships, develop a short memory.

There is no market for gloom.

Courage is the result when fear meets faith.

Test your strength by lifting a burden from another's shoulders.

What you make of your life is up to you. You have all the tools and resources you need. What you do with them is up to you. The choice is yours.

Determination is more important than talent.

Solving problems is sometimes easier than living with the solutions.

Short speeches are not always the best, but the best speeches, it seems, are always short.

If it weren't for the last minute, nothing important would ever get done.

Life is a riddle. Unfortunately, the answers are not written on the back of anything.

When criticised, consider the source.

The three secrets of success in public speaking are — be sincere, be brief, be seated.

Short visits make long friends.

Intimidation causes players to forget about teamwork and starts them thinking about their own survival. They begin talking about *my* future ... *my* safety ... *me* ... They forget about working together. Things go from bad to worse after that.

When you see a turtle on top of a fencepost, you know he didn't get up there by himself.

For the coach there is no fun in a victory that is hollow, but every thrill and joy in the game that is won against the odds.

Don't try to perform beyond your abilities — but never perform below them.

A coach will burn his bed to catch a flea.

The scene was a debate in a hotly contested political campaign. One candidate rose to respond after being harshly criticised by his adversary. After pausing, deep in thought, he said: 'I'm sorry my opponent had such nasty things to say about me. I always speak well of him. Of course, I suppose we could both be wrong.'

One of the worst tragedies that can befall a coach is to have ulcers and still not be a success.

Genius has limits; stupidity does not.

The face you have at 20 is the face God gave you. The one you have at 40 is the one life gave you. And the one you have at 60 is the one you probably deserve.

In the wrong hands, an orchestra leader's baton is just a stick.

Success is not purchased at any one time, but on the instalment plan.

The person who is sure nothing can be done is usually someone who has never done anything.

Never take action when you're angry.

Losers quit when they are tired. Winners quit when they have won.

Players and associates are inspired by confidence in their coaches. Great coaches inspire them to have great confidence in themselves.

If you wouldn't write it and sign it, don't say it.

The desk is a dangerous place from which to watch the world.

Winners expect to win in advance.

You can't steal second base and keep one foot on first.

To lead without direction is foolish and those who follow are fools.

Talk to your enemies because they will tell you your faults.

The problem with some people is that they'd rather pray for forgiveness than fight temptation.

Don't waste time learning the 'tricks' of the trade. Instead, learn the trade.

Remember that all news is biased.

Be brave. Even if you're not, pretend to be. No one can tell the difference.

Don't mess with drugs and don't associate with those who do.

Start meetings on time regardless of who's missing.

Aim at nothing and you'll succeed.

He who is content with little has everything.

Hey coach, fix the mistake — not the blame.

Flattery is telling your players exactly what they think of themselves.

The test of generosity is not how much you give, but how much you have left.

A baseball coach once rebuked a confident player who said their team would win because it had 'the will to win'. 'Don't kid yourself,' said the coach. 'The will to win is important, but it isn't worth a nickel unless you also have the will to prepare.'

Diligence is more important than intelligence.

If there exists no possibility of failure, then victory is meaningless.

The superior coach will watch over himself.

To win and keep winning, you have to pay attention to the smallest details.

Most people will agree with you — if you'll just keep quiet.

SHORT CUTS

Even a stopped clock is right twice every day.
Marie von Ebner-Eschenbach, Austrian novelist

A committee is a group of people who keep minutes and waste hours.
Milton Berle, US comic

Our greatest weariness comes from work not done.
Eric Hoffer, American philosopher

Nothing in the world is friendlier than a wet dog.
Dan Bennett, Bits & Pieces

It's only a rort if you're not in it.
Bart Cummings, Horse Racing

The nice thing about egotists is that they don't talk about other people.
Lucille S. Harper

If I just had some humility, I'd be perfect.
Ted Turner, businessman

The easiest way to make money is to stop losing it.
Robert Heller, management consultant and author

It doesn't take talent to be on time.
Pete Reiser, actor

A conference is a gathering of important people, who singularly can do nothing, but together can decide that nothing can be done.
Fred Allen, US comedian

Make yourself necessary to someone.
Ralph Waldo Emerson, US essayist and poet

The more power is divided the more irresponsible it becomes.
Woodrow Wilson, US President

Be grateful for luck, but don't depend on it.
William Feather, US publisher, author

Learn to obey before you command.
Solon of Athens, statesman, legal reformer and poet.

I never think of the future. It comes soon enough.
Albert Einstein, physicist

Adversity reveals genius. Prosperity conceals it.
Horace, Roman orator

Necessity never made a good bargain.
Benjamin Franklin, scientist and diplomat

When I am dead, I'd rather have people ask why I have no monument than why I have one.
Cato the Elder, Roman general and statesman

I told the doctor I couldn't relax. He said, 'Force yourself.'
Ron Dentinger, US humorist

With luck even a fool wins glory. Without it, a hero is helpless.
Dang Dung, Vietnamese patriot

Most people find fault like there is a reward for it.
Zig Ziglar, motivator

The desire for safety stands against every great and noble enterprise.

Make very few promises to your players and keep them all.

Smart coaches learn from their own mistakes. Smarter coaches learn from the mistakes of others.

Courage doesn't always look the way you think it does. Courage can be getting out of bed every morning or remembering to say thank you.

League standings are kept by team, not by individuals.

There are no small parts, only small actors.

The real test in golf and in life isn't keeping out of the rough, but getting out after we're in it.

Never let yesterday use up too much of today.

When you don't know what to do, do it slowly.

Stop complaining about what you don't have and use what you've got.

There's nothing wrong with underachieving. It just doesn't pay very well.

Most of us know how to do nothing. Few of us know when.

Friends … do not set traps for them. If you tempt a friend you are unworthy of friendship. Don't ask them to go out of their way to accommodate you. Don't presume on their good nature.

Always be suspicious of a subordinate who never finds fault with you.

You'll never leave where you are, until you decide where you'd rather be.

The coach herds sheep, drive cattle and leads people.

Profanity is the effort of a feeble mind to express itself forcefully.

Never ask a question you don't want to hear the answer to.

Never argue with an angry person.

An exchange of ignorance is an argument.

'If you are sent to bring something, bring it and not an explanation,' he told his players. 'If you agree to do something, do it; don't come back with an explanation. Explanations as to how you came to fail are not worth two cents a tonne. Nobody wants them or cares for them.'

The person who takes a stand is often wrong, but those who fail to take a stand are always wrong.

Never pay a compliment as though you expected a receipt.

You can tell if you are on the right track — it's usually uphill.

A SHORT 'HISTORY' OF MEDICINE

2000 BC	'Here, eat this root ...'
1000 BC	'That root is heathen, say this prayer ...'
1850 AD	'That prayer is superstition, drink this potion ...'
1940 AD	'That potion is snake oil, swallow this pill ...'
1985 AD	'That pill is ineffective, take this antibiotic ...'
2000 AD	'That antibiotic is artificial ... here, eat this root.

It takes only 10 minutes to find in others the faults we often fail to discover in ourselves in a lifetime.

Aggressive behaviour is most often motivated by fear. Assertive behaviour is most often motivated by confidence.

It takes a lot of things to prove you're smart, but it only takes one to prove you're dumb.

There is nothing more deceptive than an obvious fact.

If you find a path with no obstacles on it, chances are it doesn't lead anywhere.

Without information, it is difficult for the player to make meaningful contributions to the game.

It's not so much what the coach knows. It's how well he uses what he knows.

The rooster crows — but the hen delivers the goods.

Coaches who know all the answers usually don't understand the questions.

No one is as tired as the person who does nothing.

Hospitality is making your guests feel at home even though you wish they were.

Even the highest towers begin on the ground.

Life isn't a dress rehearsal.

If you don't know where you're going, when you get there you'll be lost.

SEVENTEEN

As Told by the Greats

'The coach can preach a better sermon with his life
than with his lips.'

I never had the ambition to be something, I had the ambition to do something.

WALTER CRONKITE, JOURNALIST AND NEWS ANCHORMAN

Life breaks us. And when we heal, we're stronger in the broken parts

ERNEST HEMINGWAY, US WRITER

He who can, does.
He who cannot, coaches.

GEORGE BERNARD SHAW, IRISH PLAYWRIGHT

You can map out a fight plan or a life plan, but when the action starts, it may not go the way you planned, and you're down to your reflexes — which means your training. That's where your roadwork shows. If you cheated on that in the dark of the morning, well, you're getting found out now under the bright lights.

JOE FRAZIER, WORLD HEAVYWEIGHT BOXING CHAMPION

NO MISUNDERSTANDING

I'd rather see a sermon
Than hear one any day.
I'd rather once you walk with me
Than merely show the way.
The eye's a better pupil
And more willing than the ear.
Fine counsel is confusing,
But the example always clear.
I soon can learn to do it
If you let me see it done.
I can see your hands in action,
But your tongue too fast may run.
And the lectures you deliver
May be very fine and true.
But I'd rather get my lesson
By observing what you do.
For a person must understand you
And the high advice you give.
But there's no misunderstanding
How you act and how you live.

Anonymous

Man often becomes what he believes himself to be. If I keep on saying to myself that I can not do a certain thing, it is possible that I may end by really becoming incapable of doing it. On the contrary, if I believe I shall surely acquire the capacity to do it, even if I may not have it at the beginning.

MAHATMA GANDHI, INDIAN CIVIL RIGHTS CAMPAIGNER

Do not confuse passion with success. Passion is the joy of getting there. Success can be a trap.

NEIL SIMON, US PLAYWRIGHT

Everybody who is incapable of learning has taken to coaching.

OSCAR WILDE, IRISH WRITER

The coach must himself believe that willing obedience always beats forced obedience, and that he can get this only by really knowing what should be done now. Thus he can secure obedience from his players because he can convince them that he knows best precisely as a good doctor makes his patients obey him also he must be ready to suffer more hardships than he asks of his soldiers, more fatigue, greater extremes of heat and cold.

XENOPHON, ANCIENT GREEK MILITARY LEADER

I am not young enough to know everything.

OSCAR WILDE, IRISH WRITER

The greatest tragedy in life is people who have sight but no vision.

HELEN KELLER, SOCIAL REFORMER AND WRITER

Live with no time out.

SIMONE DE BEAUVOIR, FRENCH WRITER

There is no doubt that it is around the family and the home that all the greatest virtues, the most dominating virtues of human society, are created, strengthened and maintained.

SIR WINSTON CHURCHILL,
BRITISH PRIME MINISTER

Criticism is something we can avoid easily — by saying nothing, doing nothing, and being nothing.

ARISTOTLE, GREEK SCIENTIST AND PHILOSOPHER

Sport has nothing to do with fair play. It is bound up with hatred, jealousy, boastfulness and disregard for all the rules.

GEORGE ORWELL, ENGLISH AUTHOR

'Dear Mr President, I received your invitation three days before I agreed to speak a few words at a dinner honouring the wonderful high school teacher who taught me to write. I know you will not miss me at your dinner, but she might at hers.'

US AUTHOR JAMES MICHENER SENT THESE WORDS OF REGRET TO PRESIDENT EISENHOWER AFTER HE WAS ONCE INVITED TO THE WHITE HOUSE

Without discipline, there's no life at all.

KATHERINE HEPBURN, US ACTRESS

You cannot shake hands with a clenched fist.

GOLDA MEIR, ISRAELI PRIME MINISTER

Success is the ability to go from one failure to another with no loss of enthusiasm.

SIR WINSTON CHURCHILL, BRITISH PRIME MINISTER

My mother said to me, 'If you become a soldier, you'll be a general; if you become a monk, you'll end up a Pope.' Instead, I became a painter and wound up as Picasso.

PABLO PICASSO, SPANISH PAINTER AND SCULPTOR

I long to accomplish a great and noble task, but it is my chief duty to accomplish small tasks as if they were great and noble.

HELEN KELLER, SOCIAL REFORMER AND WRITER

Progress was all right once, but it went too far.

OGDEN NASH, US POET

LILLIAN VERNON'S 10 TIPS FOR SUCCESS

In 1951, Lillian Vernon launched a mail-order business by placing a $500 advertisement in Seventeen *magazine to sell monogrammed leather purses and matching belts. Vernon spent $2000 on a supply of purses and belts and then personally monogrammed them after the advertisement attracted $32,000 worth of orders.*

From such humble beginnings Vernon established a business that grew into a multi-million-dollar, publicly traded, mail-order company with a catalogue circulation of more than 141 million In February 1996, Working Woman *magazine ranked her at No. 13 in the 'Top 20 Paid Women in Corporate America'.*

- Lillian Vernon offers these 10 tips for business success:
  - Make time for yourself and your family.
  - Surround yourself with the best people possible.
  - Be open to new ideas and better ways to do things. Keep all lines of communication open with your staff.
  - Be prepared to take risks.
  - Like what you do and like what you sell.
  - Don't dwell on your mistakes or setbacks — learn and grow from them and then move on. Never let your mistakes defeat or discourage you. Never take criticism personally.
  - Don't try to do it all — delegate!
  - Don't grow too fast without the proper systems and people in place to handle the growth of your business.
  - Don't be afraid of new technology that can help make your business more efficient.
  - Don't spend any more money than you have — set realistic budgets and stick to them. Keep your debts manageable.

From Pamela Boucher Gilberd's The Eleven Commandments of Wildly Successful Women *(Hungry Minds Inc, 1998)*

I really don't deserve this, but I have arthritis and I don't deserve that either.
>> COMEDIAN JACK BENNY, IN AN ACCEPTANCE SPEECH

People are always blaming their circumstances for what they are. I don't believe in circumstances. The people who get on in this world are the people who get up and look for circumstances they want and if they can't find them — make them!
>> GEORGE BERNARD SHAW, IRISH PLAYWRIGHT

Excellence is an act won by training and habituation. We do not act rightly because we have virtue or excellence, but rather we have those because we have acted rightly. We are what we repeatedly do. Excellence, then, is not an act, but a habit.
>> ARISTOTLE, GREEK SCIENTIST AND PHILOSOPHER

You are never really playing against an opponent. You are playing against yourself, your own highest standards. And when you reach your limits, that is real joy.
>> ARTHUR ASHE, TENNIS

You don't get to choose how you're going to die. Or when. You can only decide how you're going to live.
>> JOAN BAEZ, US SINGER AND POLITICAL ACTIVIST

The three rules of work:
1. Out of clutter, find simplicity.
2. From discord, find harmony.
3. In the middle of difficulty lies opportunity.
>> ALBERT EINSTEIN, PHYSICIST

Fans don't boo nobodies.
>> REGGIE JACKSON, BASEBALL

We seldom repent of having eaten too little.
>> THOMAS JEFFERSON, US PRESIDENT

Commonsense is genius dressed in its working clothes.
RALPH WALDO EMERSON, US POET AND ESSAYIST

When I've been unsuccessful, I've been controlled. When I've been successful, I've been in control.
KATHERINE HEPBURN, US ACTRESS

One important key to success is self-confidence An important key to self-confidence is preparation.
ARTHUR ASHE, TENNIS

Don't write merely to be understood. Write so that you cannot possibly be misunderstood.
ROBERT LOUIS STEVENSON, SCOTTISH WRITER

Never mistake motion for action.
ERNEST HEMINGWAY, US WRITER

Beware of entrance to a quarrel.
WILLIAM SHAKESPEARE, ENGLISH PLAYWRIGHT AND POET

Forgive your enemies — but never forget their names.
JOHN F. KENNEDY, US PRESIDENT

Our lives begin to end the day we become silent about things that matter.
MARTIN LUTHER KING JNR, CIVIL RIGHTS CAMPAIGNER

A short pen is better than a long memory.
CONFUCIUS, CHINESE PHILOSOPHER

ABOUT THE CO-AUTHOR

Ian Heads, a fan of the game from school days, wrote his first words on rugby league in season 1963, and has been around the game ever since. He was chief rugby league writer for the *Daily* and *Sunday Telegraphs* 1969-81 and managing editor of *Rugby League Week*, 1981-87. In the years since he has continued to work for newspapers and magazines, and also to author or co-author many books on sport. They include a wide range of biographies and autobiographies with Peter Sterling, Wayne Pearce, Arthur Beetson, Ken Arthurson, Noel Kelly, Malcolm Reilly, Benny Elias, George Piggins, Frank Hyde and Shane Webcke, and four treasured projects capturing the wit and wisdom of the 'Coach of the Century', Jack Gibson, *Played Strong, Done Fine*; *Winning Starts on Monday*; *When All is Said and Done*; *The Last Word*.

www.ingramcontent.com/pod-product-compliance
Lightning Source LLC
Chambersburg PA
CBHW022053290426
44109CB00014B/1086